WHEN
WOMEN
*Vote*

*Stephanie F. Donner &*
*Amber F. McReynolds*

*When Women Vote*
Published by Alden-Swain Press
Denver, CO

Library of Congress Control Number: 2019949992
ISBN: 978-1-7325377-7-4

Political Science / Political Process / General
Social science / Women's Studies

Cover and interior design by Victoria Wolf

Edited by Kathy Nelson

Stephanie Donner author photo by Evan Semon
Amber McReynolds author photo by Tommy Collier

Quantity purchases: Schools, companies, professional groups,
clubs, and other organizations may qualify for special terms
when ordering quantities of this title. For information, email
bulksales@aldenswain.com.

*For Adi, Klara, Marcus, and Kenton in the hope
that they continue to lift one another up and
advance equality for all.*

# CONTENTS

# OUR KIDS → FOREWORD

**I THINK WOMEN SHOULD HAVE** the same equality as men. Children have an opinion too. Children at age ten & nine have some strong opinions. I wish I could vote. My mom worked very hard day and night to finish the book by deadline. Stephanie and Amber were a team. They would have meetings once or twice a week and talk all the time. They have tried so hard, and it paid off. Klara, Amber's daughter and I, want to write a children's version. My favorite part of the book is the part about the Tuesday Club. You will have to read to find out why. Thank you for listening, and I hope you enjoy the book!

ADI (AGE 9)

I think women should vote because they should be able to decide for themselves. It's not fair if men only get to vote. I loved watching my mom work hard to write this book with Stephanie. This book is important because everyone should be able to vote easily. You have to show up and vote. My mom worked super hard and would stay up all night. My mom's favorite job is being our mom, and her second favorite is helping people vote. And she does this across the entire United States of America. I even go with her sometimes to give speeches. It's amazing to be by her side. Please be sure to always vote. I hope you love this book! Votes for women!

KLARA (AGE 8)

I am proud of my mommy for writing this book with her friend Amber. Women should vote because they are good guys! Women should vote because they should have the same thing that men have. My mommy worked really hard on this book and she showed perseverance making it because it is a really long book. I really liked being able to hang out with Kenton and Klara when mommy wrote the book and my daddy helped. Men and women should have the right to vote for ever. Thank you for writing this book mommy and Amber.

**MARCUS (AGE 6)**

*Marcus*

My momma works so hard. I love my momma so much. I can't wait to read the book she wrote with my friend Marcus's mom—Miss Stephanie. They did it together, and I think that is really cool. It's like when Marcus and I play baseball together. We are a team. And also there are really cool maps in the book. I like the maps.

**KENTON (AGE 6)**

*Kenton*

# INTRODUCTION

**EVERY TUESDAY**, beginning in 1910, Deborah Given set the lunch dishes in the exact same place on the large dining table in her El Paso, Texas, home. Each of her guests had assigned seating in the exact same seats every week. The meal had been planned. The deck of cards was stacked and ready for use. Every detail was perfect in advance of the Tuesday Club's arrival. Members of the Tuesday Club shared a love of companionship and social card playing but also despair that solely because they were all women, none of them could vote. The card playing and socializing provided the background to discuss women's issues and advance the then-audacious idea of a woman's right to vote. Lilian Given Braude, Deborah's sister-in-law, pressed for more women to go into business, and Deborah encouraged the Tuesday Club to organize for suffrage. With Pancho Villa directly across the Rio Grande, Deborah and Lilian were motivated to do their part, even if just in their corner of the world.

Meetings like these were held in living rooms across the country as our suffragist sisters tried to gain equal rights at the ballot box and in business. Elizabeth Cady Stanton and Lucretia Mott met one another at a tea party in New York. They ultimately took their club to Seneca Falls, New York, to kick off the suffrage movement. Other clubs designed cookbooks with campaign materials tucked inside—literal recipes for subversion. Clubs and cookbooks were the tools women used to convince husbands and political leaders to take up the cause of suffrage. To counteract the impression of masculinity, the women were encouraged to wear white dresses with sashes of purple and gold—symbolizing loyalty, purity, and life.

Change came slowly over our first one hundred years as a nation. As the western territories became states, the "Votes for Women!" battle cry spread across the region. The Wyoming legislature wrote women's suffrage into its constitution as a territory and carried that into its 1890 statehood. Three years later, in 1893, Colorado voted to become the first state in the Union to grant women

# Women's Suffrage as of 1919

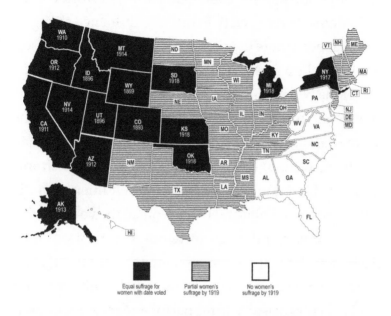

WA 1910
MT 1914
ND
MN
VT NH ME
OR 1912
ID 1896
SD 1918
WI
NY 1917
MA
WY 1869
MI 1918
CT RI
NV 1914
UT 1896
CO 1893
NE
IA
IL
IN
OH
PA
NJ
DE
MD
CA 1911
KS 1918
MO
WV
VA
KY
AZ 1912
NM
OK 1918
AR
TN
NC
SC
MS
AL
GA
TX
LA
AK 1913
FL
HI

■ Equal suffrage for women with date voted
▦ Partial women's suffrage by 1919
☐ No women's suffrage by 1919

the right to vote through a popular referendum of its all-male electorate. This kicked off a trend in western states granting female citizens the right to vote. By 1912, well before the passage of the Nineteenth Amendment, nine western states had guaranteed their (still mostly white) women the right to vote.

Since our country's founding, we have limited who could vote. A newly independent United States of America allowed only those who most closely resembled George Washington—white, property-owning men— to vote for him in our first national election in 1789. Because white men had historically been the only citizens with full entitlements, they were also the people most capable of changing the system. Women used efforts such as the

Tuesday Club and the cookbook parties to work within the parameters of society in order to influence change.

It has been more than 125 years since Colorado passed its referendum and roughly 100 years since the ratification of the Nineteenth Amendment and the achievement of national suffrage. Although women achieved the right to vote nationally 100 years ago, the process of voting has not changed enough since it was first created by men and for men. Though the Nineteenth Amendment technically gave both white and black women the vote in 1920, Native American women were not enfranchised until 1924 and Asian American women not until the 1950s.[1] Latinas were considered and included in either white or black categories. Voting parity—regardless of race or ethnicity—was not fully realized nationally until the enactment of the 1965 Voting Rights Act.[2] The voting age was not lowered to age eighteen until 1971. Even still, Mississippi did not ratify the Nineteenth Amendment until 1984.

The history of women's suffrage in the United States is complicated, to say the least. And it continues to be complicated. Hundreds of years after that first national election in 1789, the election process still operates in an antiquated way.

Barriers such as restrictive voter registration and deadlines and inconvenient or nonexistent voting options preclude many from participating in our democracy. The more barriers there are to vote, the harder it is for women to vote, especially those who are in school, have children, or are holding multiple jobs. It is difficult to find affordable childcare or to take the time required to get to the polls. Even the careers and industries dominated by women (such as teaching, nursing, retail, hospitality, and service) are the very ones with the types of schedules that do not allow personal time off for hours to stand in line or travel to vote on one set day. Women of color are especially impacted, as even higher numbers of these women work in community and social service occupations, health care, food service, and personal care.[3]

Americans who want to vote are conditioned to show up to a designated polling place, wait in a long line, and finally cast a ballot. This inconvenience is the best-case scenario. Worst-case scenarios include voters who have been cleared from the voting rolls, have gone to the wrong polling place, or have completely missed the registration deadline to begin with. A 2016 survey of unregistered voters found that most had never been asked if they wanted to register.[4] The Census Bureau estimates that at least one-third of eligible voting-age citizens remain unregistered.[5] Even when a citizen takes the time to register, the rules surrounding registration cut-off dates are confusing and not designed to put voters first.

Consider the trending conversations around making Election Day a national holiday. If a national holiday is needed in order to help more people vote, isn't every person who works disenfranchised? While many states allow voters to cast absentee ballots with no excuse required, alleviating some of the challenges of voting on Election Day, some states allow absentee ballots only for those who are disabled, elderly, in school, or deployed in the military. Eligibility to vote absentee is not an issue painted red or blue: New York and Connecticut require voters to provide an excuse in order to receive an absentee ballot, as do Texas and Mississippi.

These arbitrary barriers prevent full participation in our democracy.

Although this book singles out how women are disproportionately impacted by hurdles, our system imposes hurdles on all people, irrespective of biological sex. Specific communities face even more challenges. African Americans, for example, still face many systemic challenges due to a history of enslavement, including access to the ballot. Native Americans, immigrants, and those experiencing homelessness are all faced with inequality when trying to vote. Some states bar those who have been convicted of a felony from voting.

Inconvenient voting options limit turnout. The 2016 presidential election and the 2018 midterm election saw a record number of voters and turnout, but they still accounted for only 61 percent and 50 percent of eligible voters. And 2018 had the highest turnout for a midterm in one hundred years![6]

In an election with only 50 percent turnout, it could mean that a majority of the 50 percent (in other words, 26–30 percent of eligible voters) decide who will represent 100 percent of the population. The public's confidence in government is at an all-time low, but low voter turnout and engagement gives elected representatives little incentive to pay broad attention to the entire constituency they represent. They feel they need to care only about the people who vote.

Despite more than 40 percent of the country identifying as independent,[7] Republicans and Democrats alike engage in divisive rhetoric and partisan bickering to maintain the status quo by preaching to, and best serving, those who are perceived to be most likely to vote: their political base. Politics has become a game, with the American people on the losing side.

When all is said and done, we are not a red or a blue country but rather a no-vote country. Most states make it difficult to vote. We need to trust our elections and our elected officials so that more people will trust the work of our government. Our government will not get better until more voters vote. Today our government seems to be more at a standstill—or standoff—than anything truly functional.

We have made indelible progress as a nation to engage voters, but we can do a lot more to improve voter engagement. Solutions include expanding Vote-at-home options, early voting, automated and same-day registration, primary reform, and nonpartisan redistricting. In fact, the states that have already implemented these reforms are the states with the highest voter turnout in the nation. These are also the states with the highest women representation.

When more women are at the table (or in the voting booth), other improvements occur. Natalie Cone of the YWCA wrote in a 2019 blog post for NonProfit Vote, "Once we recognize who is not at the table, it's important to not only invite them to the table, but to also create space to let those individuals speak for and represent themselves."[8] We are already seeing how an increase of women in elected office and in business leadership is creating policies that benefit the masses—such as pay equity, improved childcare, and family leave. The playing field becomes more even and more collaborative. Women fundamentally govern differently from men.

All of this will fail to happen unless we improve and modernize our elections and the way we vote. Our election policies must put voters first and put the focus on who votes, not who wins.

To understand what the voting experience is like in different states for women of different ages, and even for those women implementing our voting systems and overseeing the election process, we interviewed a number of women and include several of their personal stories here. These women have varying political affiliations and differing racial and economic backgrounds.

They each had unique Election Day experiences. Their voting experiences represent those of millions of other people across the country. The stories of these real voters give a glimpse into what voting is like, not only for women but also for the balance of the more than 118 million people in America who cast ballots nationwide in 2018.[9] The stories also indicate how voting could be improved for us all. This book is based on those real stories. Though this book is titled When Women Vote, we have one goal in mind: highly available, high-integrity voting for all.

Let's honor what women fought for so bravely one hundred years ago. Election reform, as sexy as it sounds, is the path forward. The advice is simple: Look West.[10]

# PART 1

## WHEN WE EXPAND VOTING OPTIONS

**OUR CURRENT VOTING PROCESS** includes many barriers and excludes large percentages of voters before we even get to election day.

Cailyn walked from her apartment in a suburb of Cleveland, Ohio, to the local middle school, equal parts giddy and trepidatious, the autumn leaves crunching beneath her feet. It was Election Day.[1] Not that long ago, she was living with her parents on the other side of the city. At that point, she was on her own, working at a restaurant while going to college, balancing and blending those two parts of her life. She felt patriotic. Then she thought of her parents. Would they be proud of her? A cloud passed over her mood; her parents did not vote. No one at their church did. They did not prioritize voting because it was not a priority in their religious culture. She knew only a few neighbors, teachers, or extended family members who occasionally discussed elections. Thus, voting had never crossed Cailyn's adolescent mind. Politics and religion, like peanut butter and tuna fish, were not to be mixed. She was told not to worry about politics, and that was a good enough reason for her not to vote. Over time, as she grew up, graduated from high school, moved out on her own, and headed off to college, things changed.

"It was just one of those things that was out of sight, out of mind for me as a kid," Cailyn said as she discussed why she decided to start voting.

By the time of the November 2018 election, Cailyn, then twenty-two years old, felt a sense of ownership in her government: She was working more, and as she saw more of her hard-earned dollars going toward paying taxes, she wanted to have a voice about who was elected and the policies that they proposed.

Research suggests Cailyn is not alone in feeling a responsibility to vote. Though young adults are less likely than older people to say voting is convenient or exciting,[2] national voter turnout jumped from 2014 to 2018 by 79 percent among 18- to 29-year-olds. Young women also voted at higher rates than young men.[3]

Several states away, another woman was also gearing up to vote on the one day her state set aside for elections. Sarah felt galvanized as she gathered her belongings from her car and headed for the doors. As usual, Sarah had spent the day visiting families in East St. Louis. Her job—high touch and high stress—meant she might receive a call at any moment to jump into action on behalf of a child client, so her phone was always never more than a few feet out of reach. While her husband and their friends could go into work late or take the afternoon off to vote, Sarah had to hope she would not be called to an emergency on Election Day, which could prevent her from making it to the polls and voting.

Unlike Cailyn's civic awakening in early adulthood, Sarah's voting was a value her parents had instilled in her since childhood. Growing up, Sarah, 28 years old at the time of the November 2018 election, remembered watching the results come in on the nightly news.

"I'm a first-generation college graduate," she explained. "My mom told me growing up, 'You're going to go to college.' And I did. Now I have my master's and am a licensed social worker." Sarah received the same message from her mom about voting: she was expected to grow up to be a voter, so she is.

Although other Americans have received these same messages from their parents, many still do not make it to the polls. A survey of The Pew Charitable Trusts of registered voters who did not vote in the 2018 middterm election showed that, "41% cite inconvenience as a reason, while 30% say not being registered or eligible to vote was a reason for not voting."[4] That more than a third of these people found voting challenging is not a surprise. Even Sarah, a motivated and physically capable voter, had missed participating in some past elections due to her work schedule.

On Election Day 2018, she felt immediately reassured as she walked inside: The line was long, but at least it wasn't out the door. As she stood in line, Sarah thought back to her first voting experience ten years before, as an eighteen-year-old freshman in college, when she'd traveled across central Michigan to vote near her childhood home. The line there had been single file too, but in a tiny building in her small hometown. Sarah breathed a sigh of relief, pleased she would be able to vote well before closing time.

## REGISTRATION TRAPS

Both Cailyn and Sarah had registered to vote well in advance of Election Day. All states except North Dakota require voters to register to vote. Thirty states require

registration in advance of Election Day, and those registration deadlines vary by state. Sixteen of those states—
including Florida, Georgia, Indiana, New York, Ohio,
and Texas—require registration to occur twenty-five
or more days before Election Day.[5] Eighteen states and
Washington, DC,[6] have enacted automatic voter registration whereby eligible voters are added to the voting rolls
through transactions at government offices such as the
motor vehicles office. Further, twenty states and DC have
enacted same-day voter registration, enabling registration

## States with Same Day & Election Day Registration

Source: National Conference of State Legislatures, July 2019

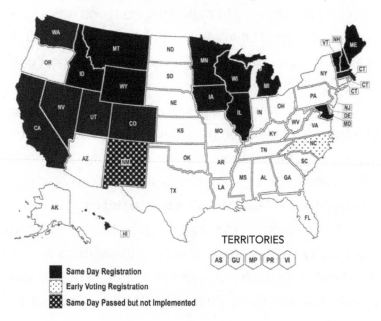

on Election Day.[7] Only ten states and DC allow for both automatic and same-day registration.

In those states that require registration in advance of Election Day, it is difficult for voters to understand the confusing registration deadlines and requirements. According to The Center for Information & Research on Civic Learning and Engagement (CIRCLE), which conducts research on the civic and political engagement of young Americans ages eighteen through twenty-nine, 87 percent of young voters surveyed in 2012 did not know their states' voter registration deadline.[8] And even once voters have figured out that deadline, it is confusing to understand how to comply.

Cailyn's circle of friends—all of them under age twenty-five—had gathered to make sure everyone was registered in advance of Ohio's thirty-day deadline. Cailyn and her friends had built their own coalition to support one another's right to vote, just as the Tuesday Clubs of the early 1900s and the suffragists had done more than one hundred years ago. Cailyn enjoyed researching the issues and relaying information, and she appreciated that none of her friends pressured her to pick sides. Cailyn was registered, educated about the ballot issues, and ready to vote.

When Cailyn got to the front of the line to vote, she was told by the election worker that the address on her ID "didn't match what's in the computer." The election worker handed Cailyn back her ID and asked her to move along.[9]

"Wait, what? What do you mean?" Cailyn replied, puzzled.

She showed up in the system, but not for that precinct. Her registration, it seemed, was for an address in Euclid, on the other side of Cleveland; the address was her parents' house. College students in Ohio can choose either to vote absentee or to make their college address their permanent address. When registering, Cailyn likely declined to make her college address her permanent address, thereby unknowingly making her voting registration address her parents' home.

"I've lived in this apartment for two years," she told the poll workers. "See? This is my address. This is my polling place." Her parents did not vote. It hardly seemed possible that Cailyn's voting would be linked to their address. She and her friends knew they needed to check to make sure they were all registered, but they never thought to confirm that the addresses listed on their registration matched their identification cards.

Five hundred and sixty miles away, Sarah was prepared to vote as well. She pulled her driver's license out of her wallet's plastic sleeve and handed it over to the late-thirties woman sitting at the table.[10]

"I can't find you," the poll worker said.

She waved Sarah off to take the next person in line. It was Sarah's first time voting at that location but not her first time voting in Missouri. Surely the woman had simply mistyped Sarah's name. Sarah asked again.

The woman checked a second time to no avail. Sarah's cheeks reddened as the election worker pulled in a supervisor. "I couldn't tell if she was mad at me," Sarah recalled, "but I felt embarrassed, and I started to cry."

Because Sarah was not in the pollbook for that polling location, the election worker told Sarah that if she wanted to vote, she would need to head across town, through traffic, to the county elections office. It seemed unlikely she would arrive there before the polls closed.

"I remember feeling like, 'There's no way I'm leaving here. I'm already at a voting location. Let me vote.'" It was all she wanted.

For Missouri voters like Sarah, registrations must be postmarked by the fourth Wednesday before the election, which for 2018 was in the second week of October.[11] St. Louis County's voter registration update form is a pdf that, although available online, cannot be filled out and submitted online. Instead, only a hard copy received by the office will be accepted.

Some states, including Missouri and Mississippi, require that registrations be postmarked by the deadline.[12] Further, requirements and timelines vary by state, which can confuse voters and make it difficult for campaigns to communicate details correctly. Thirty-seven states and the District of Columbia offer online registration, but for many the registration deadline is not any closer to Election Day,[13] which can come as a surprise to most voters. And twelve states, such as Missouri, do not allow for online registration at all.[14]

Further complicating matters, states such as Texas do not allow online voter registration, but voters can complete an online request for a paper registration form, which they can receive in the mail, fill out, and mail back. Some states use the internet as a vehicle to reinforce antiquated paper-dependent government systems. In Texas, citizens can update their driver's licenses online but must still print and mail an application to update their voter registrations.[15] This created issues in 2018, when thousands of applications were not processed because they did not have an original signature.[16]

Both Sarah and Cailyn jumped through the hoops of registration, located their assigned polling place, and then showed up to make their voices heard. Sarah, an educated, civically engaged, professional woman, was unaware of her registration status. Cailyn, a young college student motivated to vote, thought she had done everything right, but she had missed a step somewhere in a complicated process. Neither of these women anticipated the additional problems they would face once they arrived at what they thought were their respective voting precincts. They were in different states yet experienced a nearly identical challenge.

Their right to vote was limited by bureaucracy and outdated voting processes that do not favor the voter.

Determined to vote, Sarah and Cailyn were each forced to cast provisional ballots because their respective states lacked modern registration policies. Although the law requires states to notify voters regarding the status of provisional ballots, neither woman can confidently say whether her vote was counted.

The Kansas City Star, November 2018, By Lisa Gutierrez: https://www.kansascity.com/news/politics-government/article221193110.html

"I walked away feeling like they had cast it aside and were just going to throw it away," said Sarah. "I went through all that, and I'll never know if they took it or if it ended up in a pile or the garbage."

## MODERNIZING VOTER REGISTRATION

Most industrialized countries automatically add their citizens to the voter rolls, creating an opt-out process rather than the opt-in process used in the most of the United States. Many states are beginning to address burdensome registration processes and are opting for more efficient systems.

Eighteen states and the District of Columbia have already enacted automatic voter registration (AVR).[17] In states that use AVR, individuals who interact with certain government agencies and are therefore "verified" are automatically registered to vote. These individuals can choose not to vote, but because they are already registered, they can participate in elections without an extra step. In Colorado, for example, voters are automatically registered if they interact with the Colorado Division of Motor Vehicles or apply for Medicaid.[18]

Colorado is among twenty-one states plus DC that have eliminated restrictive voting registration deadlines and moved to same-day voter registration (SDR).[19] SDR eliminates barriers by allowing voters to register at the voting location and then vote on the spot. The combination of AVR and SDR is a powerful tool to support voters, including the ability to fix registration issues on Election Day.

Increasing registration options and automating the process leads more people to vote. In the five states reporting data with AVR in 2018, registration growth was nearly four times higher.[20] Oregon, the first state to implement an automatic system, has reported record turnout in every election since 2016.[21] California implemented AVR beginning in April 2018; in November of that year, it had the fifth-highest increase in turnout, jumping nearly 20 percentage points from 2014 to 2018.[22] In addition, the three states with the highest young-voter turnout all have same-day registration.[23]

There is more. States that have streamlined the registration process and use AVR for new voters have more accurate voting rolls. To further increase accuracy, seven states—Colorado, Delaware, Maryland,

Nevada, Utah, Virginia, and Washington—voluntarily banded together in 2012 to improve their voter rolls through the Electronic Registration Information Center (ERIC), which modernizes the outdated or disconnected databases that contain voter information.[24] The mission of ERIC is to "assist states with improving the accuracy of America's voter rolls and increase access to voter registration for all eligible citizens." As of September 2019, twenty-nine states and DC had joined ERIC and regularly received accurate, streamlined voter information. ERIC certifies that names and addresses are updated, locates duplicate registrations, and even identifies deceased citizens who should be removed from the registration rolls.[25]

Since many government systems do not or cannot connect with one another, participation in the ERIC system helps to eliminate the silo effect of these government databases. When people move within a city or state, election offices are informed, and then they are able to update voter registration information. States using the ERIC system also share data across state boundaries with other ERIC states. New home states are able to alert voters of their registration status or inform them of how to become a voter. This proactive approach to address updates and new registrations saves taxpayer dollars because it reduces the number of transactions a voter may need to update that voter's record, thus reducing the number of staff members required to process data changes. More importantly, it puts the voter first. Ohio joined ERIC in 2016, and Missouri joined ERIC in January 2018; however, neither Cailyn nor Sarah experienced the benefits, likely because the implementation of ERIC was not coupled with AVR or SDR, so gaps in time existed.

While Georgia has AVR and is an ERIC member state, Georgia made headlines multiple times recently for removing "non-active"[26] voters, purging more than 650,000 names in 2017 alone.[27] It seems inconsistent to automatically register voters only, to turn around and remove them. As a result of these massive purges,

## Civil rights groups sue Georgia Republican Brian Kemp over 53,000 'pending' voter registrations

By Gregory Krieg, CNN
Updated 1:55 AM ET, Sat October 13, 2018

*CNN, October 2018, By Gregory Krieg: https://www.cnn.com/2018/10/12/politics/georgia-voter-lawsuit-brian-kemp/index.html*

the number of provisional ballots cast in Georgia grew during the 2018 election and contributed to long voting lines. The Georgia example demonstrates that even though a state enrolls in ERIC and uses AVR, implementation is critical, and leadership by state and local officials is paramount to putting voters first.

The process of registering to vote does not serve the majority of voters in America. In practice, it serves political parties in an effort to identify who their voters are so that they can target them with phone calls, messages, and visits to help campaigns seek donations. Political parties, advocacy groups, associations, and even individual candidates would benefit from AVR and ERIC because the data is more accurate. States like Colorado, which has AVR and has been an ERIC member since its inception, report administrative efficiencies and more accurate address lists. States without AVR or SDR (and ERIC) force politicians and campaigns to do their work twice: first, to make sure people are registered in advance, and then to spend the next month or so convincing people to actually go to the polls. Reforms would provide tremendous benefits to all stakeholders, but most importantly to the voter.

Both Cailyn and Sarah would have been spared time, confusion, and stress if an interaction with the division of motor vehicles or post office had automatically and accurately updated their voter registrations. Yet in the 2019 legislative session, Missouri's Republican secretary of state, John Ashcroft, opposed a bill promoting automatic voter registration, despite bipartisan support. "Our concern is that by doing it automatically it may reduce the responsibility that comes with voting," a representative from the secretary of state's office said during the hearing.[28] Sarah disagrees. She took her responsibility as a Missourian seriously but still experienced barriers in the process that hindered her voting experience.

Likewise, Cailyn wants Ohio to value her vote as much as she does. She also wants young women to realize how much they are affected by the policies others enact. "I think it's important to know who's making the laws around you, who's regulating the place you work, the taxes you pay, just everything," she said. "There are so many aspects of people's lives that are affected by the laws that are being made." Cailyn looks to her government to make voting better and to ensure that what happened to her was an anomaly and not a discouraging pattern.

Unlike the situation in Missouri, in Ohio the current secretary of state, Republican Frank LaRose, has announced plans to change the state's process by "embracing technology that will improve the voter registration system" and transform "Ohio from an opt-in voter registration state to an opt-out voter registration state."[29] LaRose sees how modernizing registration to streamline the process both improves efficiency and cuts costs. "Good government" secretaries like LaRose—as well as those working to improve registration in Arizona, Maine, and Michigan—are championing better solutions for voters. Bipartisan efforts to modernize election registration to the benefit of all eligible voters would go a long way to increasing the public's confidence in elections and their outcomes.[30]

## BALLOT DELIVERY OPTIONS

For Kathy, Election Day was just like any other day. Like many women, Kathy juggles numerous, overlapping roles: Businesswoman. Mother. Churchgoer. Wife. Engaged citizen. Daughter. Sorority sister. Over the years, she's mastered the invisible labor it takes to keep all those balls in the air. As with most days, Election Day was busy. Kathy rose early to get ready for work and make the lengthy commute from her suburban home into downtown Denver. As the vice president of her division, she had back-to-back meetings scheduled for most of the day. That same long drive home awaited her when her role as a businesswoman ended for the day. Once back home, the news coverage of the election returns provided a soundtrack as she cut vegetables, asked about homework, and chatted with her husband ahead of the next day's grind.

For Kathy, voting is a sacred right—one earned by Americans who fought and died to protect our rights. She organized her own Tuesday Club in the form of sip-and-chat forums in advance of Election Day to help her local Alpha Kappa Alpha sisters learn about the candidates and issues. The women chatted online with one another from their respective homes while completing their ballots. While working on their own ballots, Kathy and her husband encouraged their preteen kids to join their conversations since they, too, would be voting in the coming years.

In Colorado, Election Day is like any other day because Colorado's ballots arrive directly in the mail weeks ahead of elections. Kathy chuckled, recalling how her mother had called nearly the moment her ballot arrived three weeks earlier. "I got mine. Did you get yours?" she had asked, all but insisting Kathy run to the mailbox to check.

Her mother had been struggling with a years-long illness. It would have been difficult for her to get to a polling place, so Kathy was relieved that being sick had not hindered her mother's enthusiastic energy for voting. Not only did Kathy's mother continue to vote, but she also conveyed that same passion to her children and grandchildren as well. Elections were not something they could afford to skip.

Kathy and her mother were afforded the opportunity to vote in advance, on their own time, and after having the time to research candidates and issues because of voting reforms passed in Colorado in 2013. Like most Coloradans, Kathy was not subject to the long lines on Election Day that dominated the headlines of the 2016 and 2018 election news cycle in many states.

Voters may expect to spend some time at the polls on Election Day, but few anticipated the kind of problems many faced across the country in the 2018 election.

---

**◥ NATIONAL**

## Long Lines Test Voter Patience Across the Nation

With waits at polling places sometimes exceeding an hour, some voters turn away as poll workers wrestle with malfunctioning equipment and overflow crowds.

by Ian MacDougall and Ariana Tobin, Nov. 6, 2018, 2:46 p.m. EST

*ElectionLand via ProPublica, November 2018, By Ian MacDougall and Ariana Tobin: https://www.propublica.org/article/long-lines-test-voter-patience-across-the-nation*

---

These issues are not new. They are not painted red or blue. And they are not specific to any one state either. Lines to vote were problematic in Philadelphia,[31] Houston,[32] Kansas City,[33] New York City,[34] and Atlanta.

Of the people Pew surveyed who planned to vote in the 2018 midterms, nearly one in seven expected it to be difficult to do so.[35] They cited long wait times, scheduling conflicts, difficulty accessing voting stations, and uncertainty surrounding how to vote, among other anticipated obstacles. So it's no surprise that only 50 percent of the voting-eligible population showed up to vote,[36] certain it was worth the trouble—including the women we interviewed and the many who stood in those long slow lines in Georgia and New York, waiting to make their voices heard.

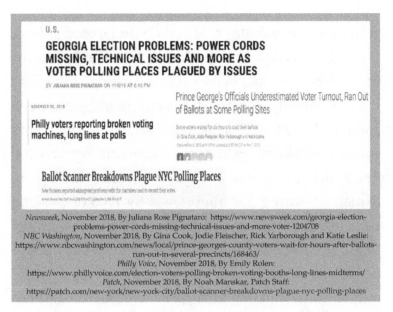

U.S.

**GEORGIA ELECTION PROBLEMS: POWER CORDS MISSING, TECHNICAL ISSUES AND MORE AS VOTER POLLING PLACES PLAGUED BY ISSUES**

BY JULIANA ROSE PIGNATARO ON 11/6/18 AT 6:13 PM

Prince George's Officials Underestimated Voter Turnout, Ran Out of Ballots at Some Polling Sites

NOVEMBER 06, 2018

**Philly voters reporting broken voting machines, long lines at polls**

**Ballot Scanner Breakdowns Plague NYC Polling Places**

*Newsweek*, November 2018, By Juliana Rose Pignataro: https://www.newsweek.com/georgia-election-problems-power-cords-missing-technical-issues-and-more-voter-1204708
*NBC Washington*, November 2018, By Gina Cook, Jodie Fleischer, Rick Yarborough and Katie Leslie: https://www.nbcwashington.com/news/local/prince-georges-county-voters-wait-for-hours-after-ballots-run-out-in-several-precincts/168463/
*Philly Voice*, November 2018, By Emily Rolen: https://www.phillyvoice.com/election-voters-polling-broken-voting-booths-long-lines-midterms/
*Patch*, November 2018, By Noah Manskar, Patch Staff: https://patch.com/new-york/new-york-city/ballot-scanner-breakdowns-plague-nyc-polling-places

Voting in America in the twenty-first century does not have to be this way.

In the days before November 6, 2018, more than thirty-six million Americans (out of the 118 million total number of voters) had already cast ballots.[37] Early voting includes absentee voting, ballots mailed to voters at home, and voting locations open in advance of Election Day. States with some form of early voting, especially mailed ballots, gain several advantages over their antiquated sister states. Getting ballots in the hands of all voters early on is one sure way to increase turnout and ensure that more women vote.

## VOTE-AT-HOME SYSTEMS

Ballots in advance of Election Day have for decades been available for military, overseas, and other voters who cannot physically vote at their designated polling places on Election Day. In the 1990s, several counties in Washington State began experimenting with offering permanent absentee status and holding elections completely by mail. The positive feedback from voters was overwhelming. Secretary of State Kim Wyman, the first Republican woman to hold the office in Washington, explained during our interview, "By 1995 or 1996, 60 percent of registered voters were voting by mail every single election. I joke now that when you hit that tipping point, you actually are a vote-at-home county or vote-at-home state and don't realize it." By 2004, the tipping point had long since passed, and the state legislature formalized the process.[38] Initially, counties could voluntarily mail a ballot to all voters, and more than two-thirds of Washington's thirty-nine counties immediately switched, as Secretary Wyman described in her interview with us. By 2010, the entire state had moved to this system. Washington was the second state to move to all-mailed ballots. The first, Oregon, saw 1.5 million Oregonians returning mail ballots for the 2000 presidential election.[39]

"I think it's really helped our voters to have a lot of options. And we don't have long lines," said Wyman.

Missouri and seventeen other states still require a specific excuse to receive a ballot in the mail.[40] Their voters must request a ballot for each election, and the exceptions and allowances for absentee voting are strict.

Across states, those exceptions include being physically out of the state on Election Day or being incapacitated by illness. Some states that require an excuse, such as Texas, will grant permanent absentee status to voters of a certain age or those with a disability, but permanent absentee status is not an option for many people who have a hard time casting a vote, such as students, those working multiple jobs, or rural voters in these states.[41]

Most states have recognized that requiring an excuse to receive an absentee ballot further disenfranchises those who want to vote. For example, Ohio voters who desire to vote their ballot at home can request an absentee ballot with no excuse prior to each election.[42] Those who request mail ballots can even track them using systems such as Cuyahoga County's VoterNotify,[43] which sends communications when ballots are mailed or received or if an issue arises. Cailyn indicated she was not aware of the absentee ballot options but also indicated that she wanted to vote in person since it was her first time casting a ballot. Recall that Cailyn chose to vote in person on Election Day and had challenges and was required to vote provisionally. Unlike voters in Ohio, any Montana voter can request permanent absentee status and receive a mailed ballot for every election thereafter.[44] This system is more cost-effective because it does not require election officials to process the same absentee requests each year.

After Oregon and Washington kicked off the all-mail

election trend, Colorado followed. As of September 2019, Utah, Nebraska, Hawaii, North Dakota, and California are expanding the use of vote-at-home options under their laws, and Montana, Arizona, Nevada, Michigan, Florida, and New Jersey are seeing increases in voters choosing to have their ballots mailed to them. The majority of Arizona's residents in Maricopa County, the fourth most populous county in the US, ask for their ballots to be delivered to them.[45] These Arizona voters are signaling to their legislators that they want more convenient voting options.

## Current Vote-at-Home Status by State—November 2019

*Map content from the National Vote at Home Institute, www.voteathome.org*

The nationwide momentum for voting at home closely resembles the suffrage movement in the late 1800s and early 1900s.

The ability to vote in advance and at home helps voters to be better informed and avoid the anxiety

# Status of Women's Suffrage by State as of 1919

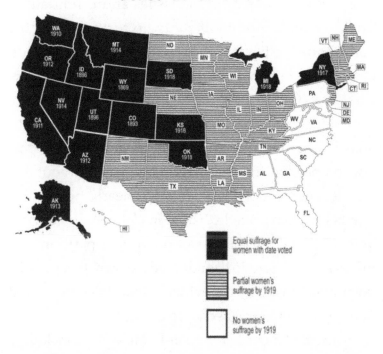

Equal suffrage for women with date voted

Partial women's suffrage by 1919

No women's suffrage by 1919

caused by long lines and other challenges voting day can bring. Colorado's ballots are often lengthy; Denver's 2018 ballot was three pages, front and back, with information in both English and Spanish—the longest ballot in the city's more than 150-year history.[46] In general, ballots are not known for simplicity either. "I work in an office that is very mixed," Kathy explained. "There are conservatives, very liberal folks, and then middle of the road, and we often exchange ideas about the things on the ballot and their perspectives." Having time with the ballot allows for more discourse with her colleagues.

A recent Emory University study found that when

ballots are delivered to voters in advance, they expend more effort researching the issues and candidates.[47] These voters are more likely to go further down the ballot and vote beyond the top races, big-name candidates, or hot-button issues. Indeed, even with long ballots, Colorado's Congressional District 2 had the second-highest voter turnout in the country (82 percent of active voters, 73 percent of eligible voters) in the 2018 midterm.[48] For comparison, Texas as a state had voter turnout that was 46.3 percent of elligible voters, nearly twenty-five points less than a single district in Colorado for eligible voters.[49] The difference is not political or partisan. The difference is Colorado has adopted a system that puts the voter first. This is further evidence that states are not red or blue, but some are just no-vote states.

States that move to a vote-at-home system, including accessible vote-at-home options, in advance of Election Day accrue several significant and undeniable benefits. Most importantly, voter turnout increases, and more people are engaged. In addition, fewer poll workers are needed, and that helps address the problem of getting poll workers—a top challenge cited by election administrators across the United States. Finally, these states save a lot of time and money. Election offices in a vote-at-home system experience reductions in call volume around Election Day, a drop in the number of provisional ballots cast, and lower taxpayer costs for voting equipment. The transformation in Colorado saved taxpayers millions of dollars.

Following the statewide rollout of mail ballots, a Pew study found costs to run elections in Colorado decreased by 40 percent overall.[50] Although supplies and labor costs can fluctuate depending on the ballot length and the number of ballots, costs still significantly shrink because fewer capital expenditures and personnel are needed to support large numbers of polling places.

Election integrity and ballot security issues are extremely important. Critics of mail ballot systems complain that they are not secure. However, states leading the trend have developed procedures and systems to ensure security, including signature verification, ballot tracking, and ballot audits. As an example, in Colorado, to ensure the election is secure and reliable, the first ballot that is received and recorded by election officials is counted. This means if Kathy chose to vote in person instead of using her mail ballot, her in-person ballot would have been recorded and her mail ballot would have been voided. There is no risk of double voting. This real-time system is a key factor in ensuring election integrity and security. When voters like Kathy move intrastate, Colorado uses data from multiple sources—including the DMV (Division of Motor Vehicles), ERIC, and address change information from the United States Postal Service—to update registration records and ensure voters still receive their ballots at their current address. Coloradans have to do very little if anything to get their ballot sent to them; it happens automatically three weeks before Election Day.

In contrast, while North Carolina offers both early voting and no-excuse absentee voting (meaning you do not need to provide a reason to request an absentee ballot),[51] voters experienced several issues with how their antiquated system is implemented. The state requires each absentee voter to find two witnesses, or a notary, to verify the voter's signature.[52] Voters are further disempowered if they miss the mail return date—ballots must be hand-delivered to the county elections office, significantly limiting voting opportunities. Instead of verifying signatures electronically and offering twenty-four-hour drop boxes, alternate mail ballot return options, or ballot tracking, North Carolina's process has made it unnecessarily difficult for voters. The state's choice to overly restrict individuals' abilities to return their ballots creates a pathway to take advantage of the rules. In 2018, North Carolina's Ninth Congressional District election was embroiled in a highly publicized ballot-tampering scandal after political operatives illegally collected, altered, and submitted absentee ballots.[53] North Carolina would be wise to focus on restricting bad actors instead of overregulating individual voters.[54]

In a world of Amazon, Lyft, Uber Eats, and many home-convenience services, it is voting—a constitutionally guaranteed right—that some states continue to forbid doing from home.

## EARLY IN-PERSON VOTING OPTIONS

Debbie had voted weeks before Election Day, taking advantage of early voting hours so she could devote her time on Election Day to supporting her political party. For this election, the party administrator had selected Debbie to be a poll watcher. It was a responsibility she was honored to uphold. Elections were serious business, and 2018 was no exception.

For Debbie, voting in El Paso County, Texas, had never been a problem. In her early years as a full-time, stay-at-home mother, Debbie had lived close enough to her precinct to put her children in a stroller and bring them along to the polls. Once she learned about early voting, participating became even easier. A lifelong voter, Debbie had become more interested in politics ten years earlier, when the youngest of her five children was preparing to leave home. She attended meetings, candidate forums, and local women's groups and then volunteered and worked with election administrators.

By Election Day, Debbie was one of the millions of Texans who had already voted. Since the Texas legislature added early voting to its election code in 1991,[55] usage has steadily grown. In the last three presidential elections, at least 40 percent of the votes cast in Texas have come through early voting.[56] This remained true during the historically high turnout of the 2018 midterms. The *El Paso Times* noted, "Nearly 4.9 million votes were cast in the 30 most populous counties when

12-day early voting ended Friday evening. That tops the total 2014 statewide turnout by 157,000 votes."[57] Early voting has been better for Debbie because she has been able to also select the most convenient voting location. If she happens to be by the library, for example, she can vote right there. Early voting is a good option because she doesn't work outside her home. Despite this convenient option for voters, Texas still has abysmal turnout, at 46.3 percent of the voting-eligible population.[58] This further demonstrates that early voting alone as a policy does not necessarily increase turnout.

## Despite Huge Improvement, Texas Voter Turnout Still Has a Long Way to Go

STEPHEN YOUNG | DECEMBER 10, 2018 | 4:00AM

*Dallas Observer*, December 2018, By Stephen Young:
https://www.dallasobserver.com/news/texas-2018-voter-turnout-still-sucked-11407128

Unlike Texas, Washington State opens its voting locations two weeks before Election Day and mails a ballot to all voters before each election. Washington Secretary of State Kim Wyman explained, "Now we have 18 days, up to and including Election Day, to solve problems instead of having one 18-hour period on Election Day." This includes assisting voters such as Cailyn and Sarah, who moved without realizing their registration was no longer valid.

"We have seen our provisional ballots, for example, go down by easily 98 percent. They are really the rare exception now," Wyman said. Washington is also implementing both automatic and same-day registration to make the process less complicated for voters.

That said, more than a dozen states, including Texas, choose to end their early voting two or more days before an election. Georgia has early voting for several weeks before an election, but the early period ends the Friday before Election Day; New York's early voting period is even shorter, beginning ten days before each election and ending two days before Election Day.[59] The fact that these states interrupt the voting process at a time when the majority of voters are paying close attention provides a disservice to the voting public.

Eleven states, including Missouri, do not offer any form of in-person early voting.[60] Sarah would have gladly taken advantage of early voting in Missouri. Because it provides more options to voters, early voting not only makes civic engagement easier on voters, it can also increase turnout among those who might not have otherwise voted. Those numbers have the potential to grow when same-day registration is also offered during the early voting period as well as on Election Day. In addition, moving away from government-assigned polling places and allowing people to vote at any voting center regardless of precinct or zip code have the potential to increase the number of voters.[61]

## CONVENIENTLY LOCATED VOTE CENTERS

A vote center is an alternative to traditional, neighborhood-based precinct polling places because you can go to any vote center to vote and you are not required to go to your assigned polling place. Vote centers give all voters—especially women—more options. Fourteen states allow for the use of vote centers on Election Day, and many more use vote centers during early voting.[62] As opposed to individually assigned polling places, vote centers expand voting options by providing more locations where people can vote that may be close to home, work, school, day care, or places that are convenient to those running errands. This method preserves in-person voting for those who prefer that experience. Further, these centers provide accessible voting options and services to voters who need assistance. Some jurisdictions, such as Denver, Colorado, Orange County, California, and Clark County, Nevada, deploy mobile vote centers to locations throughout the jurisdiction during the early voting period as well as set up vote centers at group residential facilities and nursing homes.[63] Vote centers are able to offer expanded services in fewer, more convenient locations and have real-time connectivity to the statewide voter registration database to verify eligibility and register new voters.

A vote center model—coupled with same-day registration that extends through Election Day, as Colorado and California have—would have enabled Sarah and other voters with demanding work schedules to vote.[64] Although Ohio has early voting, Ohio's model did not help Cailyn because she tried to vote on Election Day, and the system reverts back to requiring voters to go to a single designated polling place or to the county elections office to cast an eligible ballot on Election Day.

We can support citizens quite easily by expanding voting options for all voters. This includes offering early voting over a two- or three-week period up to and including Election Day, allowing voters to opt in to receive their ballot at home for all elections in every state, and expanding the use of voter-centric policies like vote-at-home systems and vote centers. Each of these solutions benefit people regardless of their political affiliation, and each is a step toward increased voter participation.

Once we improve the voting experience for all voters, confidence and trust in the process increases. Just imagine if Cailyn and Sarah had had an experience like Kathy's. Would their trust and confidence in the process have increased? Would they have become more confident in the outcome of the election and the political system overall?

## EFFECTIVE TECHNOLOGY DESIGNED FOR VOTERS

The concept of modernizing voting is not new—the Fifteenth and Nineteenth Amendments, the Voting Rights Act of 1965, and the National Voter Registration Act of 1993 are just a few examples. Despite the benefits outlined in the previous pages, some states are focused on purchasing the latest technology instead of addressing an underlying and antiquated system. After the chaos in Florida during the 2000 presidential election, Congress enacted the Help America Vote Act (HAVA).[65] Before HAVA, most of the country was still using lever or punch-card machines. Florida's butterfly ballots— whose leftover dangling paper fragment was known as the "hanging chad"—highlighted the need for improved voting systems. HAVA provided both guidelines and funding for newer, electronic machines. But many of the machines purchased with HAVA funding are now outdated and not in use, and they were also not designed to maximize accessibility, security, and usability. Thirty-eight states, more than three-quarters, use outdated and discontinued equipment.[66]

In 2018, Texas early voters reported that machines weren't properly saving selections, leading the director of elections and secretary of state to warn voters in seventy-eight counties to double-check their final votes before submitting.[67] The *Texas Tribune's* Texplainer column fielded questions such as this: "I'm hearing reports of voting machines changing the

**Tweet**

Texas Secretary of State
@TXsecofstate

TEXAS VOTERS: Please take your time & carefully review your selections before casting your ballot on eSlate voting machines. Please read our advisory & visit votetexas.gov to learn about the machine you'll be using to cast your ballot: sos.texas.gov/elections/laws... @VoteTexas

11:37 AM · 10/25/18 from Austin, TX · Twitter for iPhone

264 Retweets 188 Likes

selections of some straight-ticket voters. What gives?"[68] What gave is that those in Texas who accused the software of "switching votes" were told the problem was user error and not with the equipment itself. Texas election law does not require a paper record of the voter's choices, exacerbating the issue.[69]

Sadly, machine malfunctions continue to plague voters. In Mississippi as recently as August 2019, voters witnessed the machines flipping their votes and captured it on video.

**Voters say touchscreen machines switched their votes in nine Mississippi counties**

Numerous voting machines in Mississippi reportedly "jumped" votes — but Mitch says we don't need election security

IGOR DERYSH
AUGUST 29, 2019 10:00AM (UTC)

*Salon*, August 2019, By Igor Derysh: https://www.salon.com/2019/08/29/voters-say-touchscreen-machines-switched-their-votes-in-nine-mississippi-counties/

Beyond improved voting machines, there are various opportunities for technology to enhance the voting experience and improve processes. Ensuring that all voters have accessible voting options is paramount to an inclusive system. Further, states such as Colorado, California, and Washington have updated their technology systems to verify signatures on mail ballots; have implemented effective signature cure systems so that if a signature does not match, there is a process for a voter to cure the issue and get the ballot counted; and have instituted

ballot tracking. Several of these processes were created based on feedback from voters.

Denver implemented a ballot-tracking tool, Ballot TRACE (Tracking, Reporting, And Communications Engine),[70] after reviewing the major questions voters asked. When the data showed that one in five calls was about the status of mail ballots, Ballot TRACE launched in 2009, the first system of its kind. The system works exactly like a package tracking system: Denver voters are notified when their ballot was printed, mailed, and delivered and finally when it was returned and processed by the county. This system contributed to Denver's 86 percent reduction in calls.

Many jurisdictions, including Georgia, are replacing their electronic-only machines with those that create a

"Los Angeles County's Voting Systems for All People (VSAP) initiative is first and foremost about engaging our community and developing a voter experience that is responsive to the behaviors and preferences of our current and emerging electorate. Meeting voters where they are is a fundamental principle of the initiative. As election administrators we may not have influence over the candidates and measures on the ballot, but we have a responsibility for ensuring that the experience of voting is matched to the significance of its impact and influence. That is what a voter-centric model of voting is all about."

—**Dean Logan**, Los Angeles County Registrar of Voters

paper ballot as the official record. This is important for election security and as a method to preserve the integrity of elections in the event of a cyber attack. Paper ballots provide the means to conduct effective post-election audits and serve as the official vote. In a similar vein, Los Angeles County, California, which has more registered voters than forty-two individual states, is creating a secure touch screen-meets-paper system.[71] This system allows the voter to mark his or her choices on a screen and then print the ballot as the official record. The Voting Solutions for All People (VSAP system) was developed by the registrar-recorder/county clerk, Dean Logan, and his team in 2009 to address an aging voting system and an increasingly large and complex electorate. The project seeks a collaborative approach to voting system design that will put voters at the center and maximize stakeholder participation. Los Angeles County is the largest and most diverse county in the country, and this project focuses on the end user and stakeholder engagement and is transformational in its approach.[72]

A few states that have implemented convenient voting options have also implemented or are working to implement risk-limiting audits—driving more confidence in the electorate. The risk-limiting audit is the current recommended auditing technique for vote tabulation.[73] It is an efficient method for verifying that the outcome of the election, the reported winner, is correct. This audit technique involves manually examining a statistically meaningful sample of the votes cast. These audits have become one of the critical measures necessary to secure the election process and are a key component of a broader cybersecurity defense.[74] Risk-limiting audits are expanding in pilot form across many states, including Michigan[75] and Rhode Island.[76]

We discussed some of these voting reforms and methods with Debbie, and she had some security concerns around voting at home, mail ballots, and same-day registration. Debbie, a border town resident, has concerns about ineligible voters and believes that if Texas considered adding more mail ballot options, understanding the voter verification process for these systems would be a necessity.

"Audits have historically played a role in providing accountability for business and government entities. They help deter and detect errors and fraudulent activity as well as providing feedback for process improvement. It's time we incorporate a full range of audits into our election process! Doing so will improve the way we administer elections and inspire public confidence in the process."

—**Jennifer Morrell**, National Election & Audit Expert and Democracy Fund Consultant

Colorado, Oregon, and Washington have worked to secure the voter verification process with the most accurate address and registration lists in the country. Once ballots are returned, they undergo signature verification, through which bipartisan teams compare the ballot signature to the DMV's file as well as to signatures from past ballots and other documents. Any signatures that do not match are flagged, and two election judges, from different political parties, review to determine whether or not there is a match. If there is further concern, the voter is contacted so he or she can "cure" the ballot by providing a copy of an acceptable form of identification. Following legal challenges with the signature verification and cure processes in Georgia[77] and Florida[78] in 2018, both states have since made marginal improvements to the cure process to address these issues.

Debbie recounted an unpleasant memory from the

first time she attended ballot counting in El Paso. "They were opening the ballot box and verifying the boxes were locked. They called two people up to the box, but both of them were Democrats," she recalled. Debbie was flustered to see that verification was not done in a bipartisan manner: "They always work two and two, but it wasn't always one Republican, one Democrat." For Debbie, a Republican, parity and security are entangled.

In contrast to Texas, Colorado election judges are required to work in bipartisan teams, a best practice that should be adopted in all states, including Texas. All ballot processing areas are on camera and recorded. Every person in the area must wear a badge to indicate who he or she is and what permissions can be demonstrated. That includes outsiders who come to watch the process. The badges determine into which areas people are allowed. Finally, background checks are also required for election judges and all staff who access sensitive data or systems. This is not the case in all states, but this is a recommended best practice.

States that have implemented many of the policies discussed above have mitigated physical security risks. If a bad actor threatened a vote center or elections office, election operations and results could be impacted. If a nefarious group targeted the voting process on a single day, or if it rolled out a misinformation campaign three days before Election Day, a large swath of the population could be potentially affected. In vote-at-home states, the risk is spread out over three to four weeks. There is a public safety benefit to scattering voters and operations across multiple days as opposed to condensing everyone and everything into a single day.

According to a 2018 Pew Research Study, 67 percent of Americans think "everything possible should be done to make it easy for every citizen to vote."[79] Unfortunately, easy voting access is not often the case. Officials could (and should) investigate whether or not their state's voting experience supports voters. Ask why waiting four hours to vote is even remotely acceptable. Examine how the registration process works. Seriously question whether or not election laws—or their implementation— are voter centric.

Better policies and practices can improve the voting experience for all. Comprehensive reform includes multiple policies that work in tandem with strong implementation and security considerations. We can increase confidence by giving every eligible citizen an equal opportunity to exercise the right to vote.

# PART 2

## WHEN WE CHANGE
## THE GAME

**THINK OF OUR CURRENT** election system as a large and complicated game, with many voters excluded before they ever consider casting a ballot. Some of the most prominent games include unfair primary systems and gerrymandering. Elected officials, political parties, and election administrators often act as a siphon, excluding eligible voters through structural imbalances. This can change.

Jocelyn Benson was ready. It was not the first time she had spent Election Day anxiously waiting and longing for good news, but that night she received the news she hoped for: Nearly 53 percent of Michigan voters had chosen her to be their next secretary of state. Benson would be the fourth woman in a row and the first female Democrat to hold the role. A previous loss for the same office in 2010 made the victory in 2018 even more special, but her celebration was short-lived. Just three weeks after Election Day, political adversaries sought to strip some of her power by introducing a bill that would have, among other things, taken away her oversight over campaign-finance regulations.

> **GOP moves to dilute power of governor, AG, secretary of state**
>
> Beth LeBlanc and Jonathan Oosting, The Detroit News    Published 1:40 p.m. ET Nov. 29, 2018 | Updated 10:09 a.m. ET Dec. 5, 2018

*The Detroit News*, November 2018, By Beth LeBlanc and Jonathan Oosting: https://www.detroitnews.com/story/news/local/michigan/2018/11/29/bill-would-allow-legislators-intercede-any-court-case-involving-state/2150818002/

The three women who had been elected to Michigan's top offices, all Democrats, had not even taken office yet. Luckily, the legislation attempting to limit the secretary's independent discretion never made it out of committee, and the legislation attempting to strip authority from the attorney general was vetoed by the outgoing governor, Rick Snyder, a Republican.

When she was sworn in on January 1, 2019, Benson called it the "honor of her life. . . . I'm not a partisan person; I didn't come here to harm one party or make it hard for anyone to vote or participate in this process." During our interview, Benson's passion and frustration came through.

Partisan gamesmanship impacts the confidence the American people have in the voting process. Election results, election policies, and election administration are fraught with political influence that is geared toward who wins, not who votes.

These games have been played throughout history. We need look no further than the suffrage movement. Historically, we have viewed our voting struggles as mostly related to ballot access—who votes and how they vote—but the surrounding structural systems are also ready for and deserving of change.

The major pieces in the voting game are primary elections and gerrymandering. Primary election reform options and redistricting proposals are unfortunately fueled by partisan division. It will take a new, multipronged strategy to do away with the games that are played.

## PRIMARY ELECTION REFORM

Debbie religiously reads her *El Paso Times*. The election week edition made her pause and reflect, as something had caught her eye: a sample ballot for readers to contemplate choices before the upcoming election. It was not the existence of the ballot itself that drew her attention; it was the lack of choices. Next to a list of candidate names were mostly Ds.

El Paso, a traditionally Democratic stronghold in Texas, does not offer many opportunities for Republican voters like Debbie. "Nobody knew Republicans existed because most of our candidates are Democrats," explained Debbie. Though Texas has a semi-open-primary that permits Republicans to vote in a Democratic primary, the voter still has to request a certain party's ballot. In Debbie's case, although she could vote in the Democratic primary, she would then be denied a Republican primary ballot. In other words, Debbie would have to choose to vote only for Democrats and would be excluded from voting for any Republicans even at the local level. Her choice was limited.

In an "open primary" system, voters can choose to participate in a primary election regardless of their party affiliation. Nineteen states have open presidential primaries, and sixteen states have open state primary systems.[1] Additionally, the term *open* can have different technical requirements, depending on the particular state rules and regulations.

In states like Texas and Colorado, however, the primaries are not completely open because voters like Debbie still have to choose to select one of the major party's ballots and cannot pick and choose between candidates or parties. This denies the voter the opportunity to select the candidates who most align with her or his values and instead forces the voter, once again, to pick a side in a two-party system. Further, in some states, including Colorado, an unaffiliated voter's selected ballot choice (R or D) is then reported in the voter's public voter file for anyone, particularly political parties, to see and use. Public disclosure of the voter's choice was mandated by the legislature as a modification to what citizens passed to create the open primary system.[2] This is an intentional procedure with bipartisan support because it confers an advantage on both parties. The parties want to know who their likely voters are, as they want to reach out to them for financial contributions and with targeted campaign information. Thus, the major parties advocate for laws and policies to supply them with this information even though it may discourage participation.

## Unaffiliated? You can vote in Colorado's 2018 party primaries. But should the party you choose be public information?

By Corey Hutchins · May 1, 2017

*The Colorado Independent*, May 2017, By Corey Hutchins: https://www.coloradoindependent.com/2017/05/01/colorado-unaffiliated-vote-primary-governor/

Today, more than one-third of the American electorate, who are either unaffiliated or identify with a third party, are left out of the primary process in most states. It is no surprise that turnout for primary elections is some of the most dismal. Primary elections feel even less fair to voters who live in areas dominated by a differing party and to those who are gerrymandered into partisan blocs. The imbalance creates a disincentive for voters like Debbie to participate, even when they can. As Jeremy Gruber, Michael A. Hardy, and Harry Kresky note in their article for open primaries, "Though nowhere mentioned in our Constitution, the two major political parties occupy the dominant position in our electoral system. And when it comes to the voting rights of unaffiliated voters, now the largest group of voters in the country, there is also bipartisan unity over blocking their participation in primary elections unless allowing them access to the primary will benefit the parties."[3]

Minnesota is an open primary state with nonpartisan registration, meaning that voters are not asked to affiliate with a party when registering to vote in the primary; the option is simply not there. Thus, voters are not labeled in a specific way or divided politically. They are, however, required to choose one party's ballot when they vote, but that choice is not disclosed in the public voter file as it is in states such as Colorado. Minnesota has chosen to protect voters' privacy in that way, with Secretary of State Steve Simon advocating to prevent public disclosure.[4] He wrote in May 2019, "That's wrong, and I am doing everything possible to protect the privacy of your vote. This sort of back-door party registration system is something we've never had in Minnesota."

Reforming the primary election process provides an opportunity to improve access, enhance fairness, and encourage more competition. A movement is beginning, with states choosing to further reform primary systems and use alternative methods to vote. In addition to open primaries, ranked-choice voting is one such option. A nonpartisan or top-two primary is another.

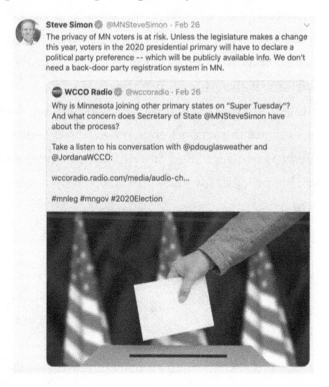

Steve Simon ☑ @MNSteveSimon · Feb 26
The privacy of MN voters is at risk. Unless the legislature makes a change this year, voters in the 2020 presidential primary will have to declare a political party preference -- which will be publicly available info. We don't need a back-door party registration system in MN.

WCCO Radio ☑ @wccoradio · Feb 26
Why is Minnesota joining other primary states on "Super Tuesday"? And what concern does Secretary of State @MNSteveSimon have about the process?

Take a listen to his conversation with @pdouglasweather and @JordanaWCCO:

wccoradio.radio.com/media/audio-ch...

#mnleg #mngov #2020Election

## RANKING OUR CHOICES

Today, voters are presented with fewer choices on their ballot. In winner-take-all-elections, "spoiler candidates" are ridiculed, and voters are often forced to choose the lesser of two evils instead of choosing their true preference. Turnout in primary elections is abysmal; thus, a small portion of the population often chooses the candidates who will be in the general election. Fair Vote's website says, "Voters nationwide are foreclosed from full participation in the democratic process because those running in the election do not present meaningful choices for voters."[5]

A ranked-choice system requires a candidate to receive 50 percent or more of the vote to win. If a candidate wins a majority of first-choice votes, he or she wins the election. If that does not happen, the votes for the candidate with the lowest number of first-choice votes is eliminated and the second-choice votes on those ballots are lifted to be recalculated among the remaining candidates. This process continues until a majority selection is reached.

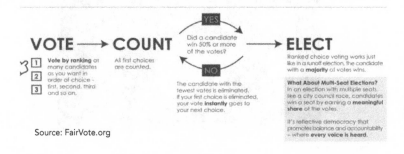

Source: FairVote.org

Because voters literally rank their choices from most preferred to least, they get a say in any subsequent retallying. Countries such as Australia, Ireland, and Northern Ireland have been using this system since as early as 1918.[6] In the US, ranked-choice is used most often in municipal elections, for military and overseas voters during an election, and for the Academy Awards.[7] In 2018, Maine used the system for both its primary and general elections, and the first member of Congress to be elected by ranked-choice voting joined the congressional freshman class of 2019.[8]

In city councils where ranked-choice voting has been used, women's representation has increased.[9]

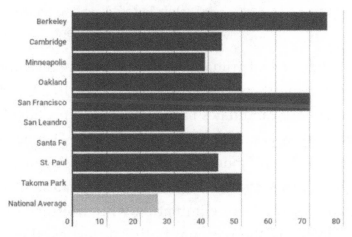

**Women's Representation on City Councils Using Ranked Choice Voting (2018)**

Ranked-choice voting is a partisan-neutral tool to eliminate split votes, fuel civility,[10] expand representation outcomes, and ensure winners have support from the majority of voters.

---

WEB ONLY / VIEWS • JULY 9, 2019

## Ranked Choice Voting Is On a Roll: 6 States Have Opted In for the 2020 Democratic Primary

We can get rid of the "spoiler" effect and make our elections more democratic. In fact, it's already happening in states across the country.

BY DAVID DALEY

*In These Times*, July 2019, By David Daley: http://inthesetimes.com/article/21959/ranked-choice-voting-2020-democratic-primary-maine-kansas

"Jurisdictions with ranked-choice voting are electing more women to office in part because campaigns are more civil, which attracts more women candidates. Multiple women can run without splitting each other's vote and running for office costs less when primaries or runoffs are consolidated into one high-turnout general election."

—Cynthia Terrell, Executive Director,
Represent Women

Presidential primaries are an interesting case study for the merits of ranked-choice voting. In 2016, the number of candidates in the Republican presidential primary was similar to those in the 2020 Democratic primary—with more than twenty candidates in each. The final selection is determined through a slow and painful process of elimination with arbitrary rules dictated by the national political parties, thereby enabling candidates to advance in each state without winning a majority. At the end of this gauntlet, the voters grudgingly must accept the last person standing to be the nominee. Presidential primary winners have not traditionally been those with the majority of the vote. In 2020, we will be able to see the impact of ranked-choice voting in some states, including Iowa, Nevada, Hawaii, Kansas, Alaska, Maine, and Wyoming during the Democratic presidential primary.[11] This could provide a roadmap for the 2024 presidential nomination process.

## TOP-TWO PRIMARY METHODS

Washington and California[12] have implemented the top-two primary system. In top-two primary systems, the two candidates with the most votes, regardless of party, move on to the general election. A single ballot includes the candidates from all parties. Everyone receives the same ballot, no matter that person's party affiliation. Proponents of top-two primaries argue it allows for the possibility of more independent or third-party candidates.

Just as Washington state was an early adopter of all-mail ballot delivery, Washington was also the first to implement a top-two primary system. In 2004, nearly 60 percent of Washington voters chose to make the switch to top-two.[13] California adopted the system after a majority of voters approved it in 2010.[14] Since then, California has had a few elections where two candidates from the same party faced off in the general election, such as the 2018 election for lieutenant governor. Two Democrats ran a close race, resulting in the election of Eleni Kounalakis, the first woman lieutenant governor of California.

Critics point out that in states with dominant single-party strength, as in Democrat-heavy California, the two candidates qualifying for a general election ballot under this method may both be Democrats. When multiple candidates of one party split the vote, it can lead to two candidates of the same party advancing to the general election.

Comparatively, the traditional primary process drives voter apathy because people like Debbie feel like their vote does not matter. Though Debbie is a Republican in an area where more Democrats vote, with a different primary system she could pick the candidate whose values most closely align with her own even if that candidate was affiliated with another party. In a ranked-choice primary, she could rate her candidates in order of preference. She would get a voice.

## ANTI GERRYMANDERING LAWS

The national Democratic and Republican parties are not the only factors creating a filter for voters during primary elections. Partisan redistricting, also known as gerrymandering, is an obvious example of the games pervasive throughout the American political system that exclude voters before Election Day. When 86 percent of seats in the US House of Representatives are not representative of the population or competitive, something is decidedly amiss.[15] The concept of redistricting is simple enough: after the Census, the states are tasked with drawing congressional district maps based on population changes.

Gerrymandering happens when the party in power chooses to tortuously redraw these districts to create a favorable map for itself going forward. It is a game both sides play to the detriment of their constituents, including the 38 percent[16] of voters nationwide who do not identify with a political party.

Districts should be drawn to be representative without regard for political affiliation or performance.

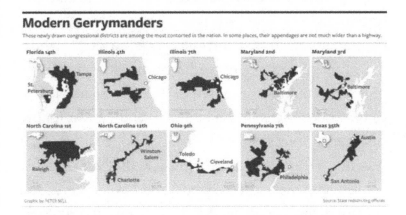

**Modern Gerrymanders**

These newly drawn congressional districts are among the most contorted in the nation. In some places, their appendages are not much wider than a highway.

Georgia's districts are a prime example of why the parties have little interest in making these districts fair. One *Atlanta Magazine* headline read, "How redrawing districts has kept Georgia incumbents in power."[17] Whoever has the power wants to keep it, without regard to the actual constituency of the district.[18] In other words, it's how the game is played.

Because gerrymandering keeps specific people or political parties in power, it also silences the voices of others who live in that district. It deters more people, including unaffiliated voters, from having a seat at the table. All laws in Georgia are created in the state legislature, as voters do not have the power of citizen-led initiatives, which are options in states such as California, Colorado, and Washington. Thus, the only voice Georgia voters have in the laws that govern them is through their elected representatives. Those same voters do not truly get a fair say in whom they elect because the major parties have drawn the districts to ensure that only certain candidates or certain parties can win.

Stacey Abrams, a former gubernatorial candidate and past minority leader of the Georgia House of Representatives, tweeted,[19] "If leaders can silence Georgians' voices at the ballot box, they can ignore Georgians' voices when in office." If politicians are not listening to the voters they represent, they are certainly not listening to the people who never have or never will vote for them. Nor would they want to give those people a chance to vote for someone else. The game continues.

Ironically, our current system allows politicians to choose their voters rather than voters choosing their politicians. Many voters who conclude that their vote does not count do not vote at all. The maps in several states, including those drawn by Democrats in Maryland and by Republicans in North Carolina, have been challenged in lawsuits and were recently heard by the US Supreme Court. In each case, the US Supreme Court ruled that federal courts should not be the final say in deciding political questions, such as whether or not districts are gerrymandered.[20] In the North Carolina case, Chief Justice John Roberts wrote for the majority that states and Congress could pass laws to prevent politically oriented districts, but asking the courts to do so would be "an unprecedented expansion of judicial power."[21] In the dissent, Justice Elena Kagan wrote, "For the first time ever, this Court refuses to remedy a constitutional violation because it thinks the task beyond judicial capabilities."

## Supreme Court allows gerrymandering in North Carolina, Maryland, setting back reform efforts

The justices found that the "partisan gerrymandering claims present political questions beyond the reach of the federal courts."

*NBC News*, June 2019, By Pete Williams: https://www.nbcnews.com/politics/supreme-court/supreme-court-allows-gerrymandering-north-carolina-maryland-n1014656

## FAIR REDISTRICTING LEADS TO FAIR REPRESENTATION

In the absence of legislative leadership, citizens are driving change. Twenty-one US states have some form of nonpartisan or bipartisan redistricting commission. Of these, thirteen use redistricting commissions to draw electoral district boundaries. Nearly all of them in the West have independent redistricting commissions in which a nonpartisan group draws the maps. After the Supreme Court ruling, Maryland's Republican governor said he would like a nonpartisan committee to draw the lines in the absence of action by the US Supreme Court.[22] Unlike traditional redistricting policies, these commissions operate in an open and transparent process.

In creating the nonpartisan commissions, some states include party registration data as part of the consideration for appointment on the commission; others expressly forbid including this as part of determining who participates on the commissions. In all cases, elected officials have limited participation, and the committees are made up of citizens from varying backgrounds. A few states, including Iowa and Utah, take a hybrid approach whereby an independent commission creates the maps; however the legislature votes to approve them.

The idea behind these commissions is not new—Montana, Idaho, Washington, and Alaska all created theirs before the year 2000—but as citizen confidence has diminished, the idea of nonpartisan redistricting is gaining steam. Voters in four states—Colorado,[23] Michigan,[24] Missouri,[25] and Utah[26]—passed independent redistricting amendments in 2018. Unfortunately, Missouri's law is already under fire, as the state's legislature wants to repeal it.[27] When legislators try to immediately undo the will of the people, it's no wonder citizens feel like their votes don't matter.

The nonpartisan nature of independent redistricting commissions helps to increase voter confidence. The electorate craves transparent and nonpartisan practices: "Most Americans Want Limits on Gerrymandering," says part of one headline for a September 2017 article regarding a national study by Campaign Legal Center.[28] Independent redistricting commissions are cited as a principal solution. The maps drawn by nonpartisan commissions result in

districts that include a more fair representation of both independent and third-party voters and are also shown to encourage political competition.[29]

Because the creation of these commissions has come mostly from ballot initiatives, voters in these states have claimed stronger, more consequential voices as to who should represent them: first by ensuring their districts are not gerrymandered and later by actually choosing which candidates are elected.

Many of the nonpartisan commissions we have discussed came about through citizen-initiated actions. Citizen-initiated actions can empower voters to engage in a dual legislative process in which both elected representatives and citizens can pass laws. This direct democracy—which voters in Colorado and twenty-five other states can employ—fosters constituents pushing for

## States with initiative or referendum

Source: Ballotpedia

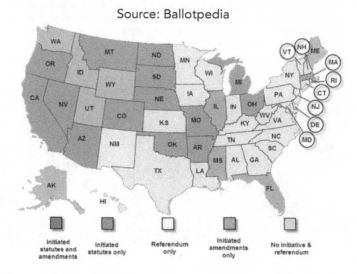

| Initiated statutes and amendments | Initiated statutes only | Referendum only | Initiated amendments only | No initiative & referendum |

ballot initiatives their legislators refuse to bring forward or are unable to pass. This mechanism is also rooted in women's suffrage. For example, when the Colorado legislature failed to pass suffrage in 1877, Colorado's male citizenry instead passed a ballot initiative to grant women equal voting rights in 1893. In the twenty-four states where no initiative or referendum power exists, voters have less opportunity to push for reforms and are solely reliant on their elected legislators for all policy decisions. While citizen-initiated actions can be costly and cumbersome, they may be a necessary tool in the absence of legislative action.

"It's up to voters to end gerrymandering," the *Washington Post*'s editorial board pleaded in 2016.[30] The Supreme Court decision in the Maryland case made it clear that voters cannot rely on the federal courts to be referees in this game; they must advocate for legislation at the state level. The crop of new laws from the 2018 election cycle shows voters are beginning to heed that call.

One of Secretary of State Benson's big tasks will be to implement and support Michigan's new independent redistricting commission.[31] The commission, which will draw districts for US Congress and state house and senate districts, will begin following the results of the 2020 Census. The new maps will go into effect in time for elections in 2022. Benson, who was inspired by the Voting Rights Act to attend law school and become a voting rights attorney, believes the transparent and effective maps the commission is expected to create could become a model for other Midwest states to follow.

Redistricting policy has traditionally been focused on who wins and not on who votes. Modernizing how we accomplish redistricting gives both citizens and legislators opportunities to fix the structural issues that work to rig the electoral game. Independent redistricting commissions benefit the electorate—and not necessarily the elected—generating representative participation. When people across the political spectrum are able to participate, they select candidates who are more representative of their views. And when voters see candidates elected who are like them, they themselves are more likely to consider running for office.

Further, meaningful change will come when there are fair redistricting and fair election processes. As Fair

Jocelyn Benson
@JocelynBenson

We're live! Yesterday we launched a two week public comment period on our proposed application to serve in the Michigan Citizen Redistricting Commission. Check it out and share your feedback at RedistrictingMichigan.org #MapMichigansFuture

9:01 AM · Jul 19, 2019 · Twitter for iPhone

Vote describes, "Winner-take-all systems in which only one person is elected to represent each district no longer work in this era of divisive partisanship across geographic and racial lines. It locks most voters into congressional districts that are increasingly skewed toward one party, safe for the incumbent, and leaves so many voters unrepresented and powerless to affect outcomes. Multiseat districts enable fair representation for multiple constituencies of color, women, or ideological minorities."

The Fair Representation Act at the federal level,[32] if passed, would combine independent redistricting commissions with ranked-choice voting and multiseat districts.

Balanced participation creates balanced representation. Trust in elections drives trust in government.

# PART 3
## WHEN WE ELECT MORE WOMEN

**THE STATES THAT HAVE IMPLEMENTED** many of the reforms advocated for in Parts 1 and 2 are the states with the highest womens' representation.

When Republican suffragist Jeannette Rankin of Montana was elected to the US House of Representatives in 1916, four years before the ratification of the Nineteenth Amendment, she became the first woman to serve in Congress.[1] It was no coincidence that she won in the first election after Montana granted its white female citizens the right to vote. (Native women would wait another ten years to be able to vote.) Rankin won because women could vote for her and because there were three candidates running for two at-large seats.[2] More voters and a top-two system led to her victory.

Jeannette Rankin was the first, last, and only woman from Montana elected to federal office.[3]

Progress has been slow. Some seventy-six years later, 1992 would be dubbed the "Year of the Woman" after women gained twenty-two seats in Congress.[4] Though representation increased by 5,300 percent from Rankin's historic win, women held only 54 of the 535 seats in the Year of the Woman—or about 10 percent of congressional seats.

Even with the "pink wave" of 2018, only 24 percent of congressional seats were held by women as of September 2019.[5] Republican women hold 21 of the 127 seats held by women overall.[6] And despite the Pink Wave, there are still 12 states without any women in Congress—including Vermont, which has yet to send a woman to serve in Washington, DC.[7]

**TODAY WOMEN MAKE UP**

**24% of Congress**

**21% of mayors of large cities**

**18% of governors**

**29% of state legislatures**

While it is encouraging that there are more women in the US Congress than ever before, their numbers amount to just a quarter of overall seats.

The numbers at the state level are similar. Only

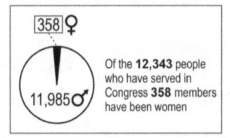

Source: Represent Women, July 2019

nine of the fifty states have women governors.[8] Of the nine governors, six are Democrats and three are Republican women. A quarter of female state legislators are women of color, and only five states have legislatures in which women are 40 percent or more of the membership.[9] According to the Center for American Women and Politics at Rutgers University, women hold nearly 28 percent of the executive positions at the state level and 29 percent of the seats in state legislatures.[10] A quarter of female state legislators are women of color, and only five states have legislatures in which women are 40 percent or more of the member-ship.9 In the hundred largest cities, only 20 percent have female mayors.[11]

The United States ranks behind seventy-six countries for

women's political representation, according to the Inter-Parliamentary Union, which ranked countries according to the percentage of women in each country's lower house.[12]

**RepresentWomen's 2019 International G20 Tracker**

# United States

**78th**

Women's representation ranking

Women now hold 102 out of the 432 (23.6%) seats in the American House of Representatives

## How is the U.S. Approaching Parity?

*The United States has no official gender quota. Only nine out of the 50 governors in the United States are women and 26% of senators are women. The country has yet to pass the Equal Rights Amendment, which guarantees equal legal rights regardless of sex.*

Lower house

% women in the American Congress

1997 1999 2001 2003 2005 2007 2009 2011 2013 2015 2017 2019

REPRESENT WOMEN

Information from IDEA, IPU

It is not a coincidence that the top four states with the highest number of women representatives (Nevada, Colorado, Oregon, and Washington) have many of the voter-friendly laws discussed throughout this book, such as modern registration policies, expanded early voting, convenient opportunities to vote before or on Election Day, open primaries, and fair redistricting

# Women's Representation by State

Source: National Conference of State Legislatures,
Kate Rabinowitz/Washington Post

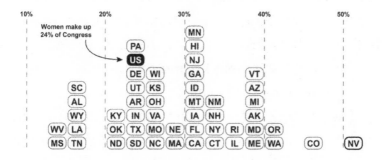

processes. These were also the same states that led the way in the women's suffrage movement beginning in 1869. Colorado elected its first three women to the Colorado General Assembly in 1894, the year after Colorado suffragists achieved the right to vote.

Washington's secretary of state, Kim Wyman, represents one of the top states for women's representation and voter-friendly laws. In the late 1980s, marriage took her from the West Coast of the United States to the middle of Bavaria, Germany. Moving from a place rooted in the twentieth century to one in the eighth century was a bit of a change, but she was proud of her Army Ranger husband and the country he served. Letters from home and trips to the mailbox became part of her everyday routine.

Election season that year was quite disappointing for Wyman. She and her husband had completed the necessary paperwork to ensure they would still be able to vote absentee during their time stationed overseas. But their ballots arrived the day after the election.

"Oh well," she thought, and she continued to sort through the remaining mail.

The nagging feeling of disappointment, however, wouldn't go away. Soon the annoyance in the back of her head lit a fire in her belly. She had never missed an election before, not since first voting for Ronald Reagan as an eighteen-year-old. Wyman realized how important voting was to her; it was something she hadn't recognized until she was denied the opportunity. This newfound knowledge set her on a different path in life.

In 1991, the Army moved her family to Washington State, and Wyman began working in the Thurston County Auditor's Office. It wasn't long before she was promoted to county elections manager.

"I made a commitment to myself that no voter in my charge would ever experience what I did," explained Secretary Wyman during our interview. Secretaries Benson and Wyman share a passion for voting that stems from the voting experience they had while their husbands were serving in the military. Benson said she was inspired to run for the office again when she found her husband's ballot—he was deployed in Afghanistan during the 2012 election—which had been returned and stamped "undeliverable" after Election Day.

Today, both of Washington State's US senators are women. The governor and attorney general of Oregon are women, and women make up 47 percent of the Colorado General Assembly.[13] Women in Nevada hold 52 percent of their state legislature, making Nevada the first and only state where women in the legislature outnumber men. In addition, two-thirds of the state's US congressional seats are held by women.[14]

Comparatively, states such as Texas, Missouri, Ohio, and Georgia don't come close to cracking the top ten states for women in office. In the Georgia state legislature, 31 percent of the seats are held by women. Women make up only 27 percent of Ohio's state legislature and 16 percent of its federal congressional delegation. Missouri women hold only

Tweet

RepresentWomen
@repwomen

.@repwomen created the #GenderParityIndex to track women's representation at the local, state & federal level & to better understand why some states are electing more women - states with #MultiSeatDistricts, for example, elect twice as many women to office #RulesMatter4Parity

RepresentWomen's 2019 Gender Parity Index

10:32 AM · 5/18/19 from Takoma Park, MD · Twitter for iPhone

25 percent of seats in the state legislature.[15] As we identified in part I, Ohio's and Missouri's existing registration processes are not overly voter friendly, and improvements are still needed. Though Georgia and Texas have made what should be positive reforms, the implementation of

these reforms actually excludes voters.

When more women vote, more women are encouraged to run. When more women run, more women are elected. And when more women are elected, women—who account for nearly 51 percent of the US population[16]—have a louder voice.

Women are not a special interest. We are an interest of half the country.

## MORE FOCUS ON WOMEN'S ISSUES AND MORE COLLABORATION

Women govern differently than men do in some important ways. Women legislators sponsor more bills, pass more laws, and send their districts more money, according to a study in the American Journal of Political Science.[17] Men are more likely to propose bills in agriculture, energy, and defense. Women are more likely than men to sponsor bills in areas such as health, education, and individual rights, which are more likely to benefit women and children. An October 2018 article by Craig Volden and others in the journal *Political Science and Research Methods* confirmed this after analyzing 151,824 public bills introduced in the House between 1973 and 2014.[18]

The 2019 Nevada legislative session is a prime example. In Nevada, the only state with majority women in the state legislature and a state that has implemented many of the voting reforms discussed here, women introduced bills such as adding an Equal Rights Amendment to the state constitution, banning child marriage, creating a review panel to research maternal mortality, and supporting the mental health of children.[19] Outside of the legislative session, Nevada voters championed women-friendly policies. "I don't think it's any surprise that those are the kinds of topics that got attention, because when you have that many women serving in the Legislature, they know that those are kind of critical life or death, or at least economic prosperity issues, for women," said Nevada State Senator Julia Ratti in an interview with the *Las Vegas Review-Journal*.[20]

# Nevada's majority-female legislature changing the conversation

**By** John Sadler (contact)
**Friday, May 31, 2019 | 2 a.m.**

*Las Vagas Sun*, May 2019, By John Sadler: https://lasvegassun.com/news/2019/
may/31/nevadas-majority-female-legislature-changing-the-c/

Colorado has experienced similar policy shifts as it has reformed its voting process. Of all the states, Colorado has the second-highest number of women in its state legislature. In 2019, Colorado women sponsored legislation to address pay equity, improve retirement savings, and provide paid family leave, among other women- and family-centered policies.[21] The Equal Pay for Equal Work Act was signed into law in June 2019.[22] The same legislative session yielded a law providing funding for full-day kindergarten and another to make sexual harassment complaints against elected officials a part of the public record.[23] A bill to create a twelve-week paid family leave insurance program did not pass but became a feasibility study.[24] Colorado passed a bill sponsored by a woman representative to provide menstrual hygiene products to women who are in custody in county jails immediately and free of charge.[25]

Contrast Nevada and Colorado with states such as Mississippi and Indiana which do not have many of the positive voter reforms discussed throughout this book. No woman from Mississippi had ever served in the US Congress until Cindy Hyde-Smith was appointed (not elected) in March 2018.[26] A lack of representation continues into the state legislature, where Mississippi ranks forty-fifth, with only 14 percent of seats held by women.[27] And Mississippi policies reflect the low number of women elected officials. Mississippi has the lowest life expectancy[28] and the highest infant mortality rate of any state, and those issues could be addressed with policies focused on women and children.[29]

It's no surprise; voting is not easy in Mississippi. Voter registration in Mississippi is paper based. Though residents who are already registered can update their registrations online, any new registrations must take place via a paper application. These applications are due thirty days before an election. An excuse is required for anyone who desires an absentee ballot. Mississippi does not offer early voting. Mississippi, despite being the birthplace of suffragist Ida B. Wells, did not ratify the Nineteenth Amendment until 1984.[30] Only thirty-six states were needed to ratify, which happened by August of 1920, so Mississippi just took its time.

Similarly, only 23 percent of the Indiana legislature are women, and among Indiana's thirty-one largest cities, there is only one female mayor. As of 2018, in terms of pay equity, Indiana ranked forty-eighth in the nation, and Hoosier women earned only seventy-three cents for every dollar earned by a man.[31]

How is it to vote in Indiana? Indiana has strict voter registration deadlines, and you must reside in your precinct thirty days prior to Election Day and be registered to vote at least twenty-nine days prior to Election Day. Indiana is also one of seven states that has significant restrictions on absentee voting. Similar to Mississippi, to simply receive a ballot in the mail, you must be over sixty-five, have a disability, be confined in a hospital, be committed to work for more than twelve hours on Election Day, be a member of the military, be a serious sex offender, or be restricted due to religious considerations, to name just a few.[32] So it is no surprise that Indiana ranked fortieth in turnout in the 2018 general election, slightly ahead of Mississippi, which ranked forty-seventh.[33]

## MORE WOMEN = BETTER COLLABORATION

Women also bring a collaborative leadership style that tends to be more democratic than men's more autocratic style. Research has found that women interrupt less but are interrupted more. They pay closer attention to other people's nonverbal cues, often achieving consensus earlier.[34] "Women have the great potential to govern differently," says Lyn Kathlene, a political scientist who studies gender and governing and and served as director of Spark Policy Institute. "But my expectation is that's going to be less overt than behind the scenes, because the reality is you have to play the game as the game's played."[35] Working within the system in order to change it, Nevada Republican Assemblywoman Heidi Gansert told the *Las Vegas Review-Journal* that having more women "lent to an environment where we had more collegiality and collaboration, and while we didn't agree, colleagues treated each other very respectfully. The partisanship was significantly reduced in this environment. So we disagreed on the issues, but everybody treated each other extremely well."[36]

Wyman believes that she must approach her role as secretary of state in a similarly collaborative way. Election administrators make the decision of where to locate polling places or vote centers, how many places are needed, what early voting hours will look like, and the kind of communication their residents will receive.

All of this heavily impacts the voting experience. "And if we can't instill that confidence in voters, then we're putting our democracy at risk," said Wyman. "That's my biggest frustration right now—on both sides—is that people are willing to burn it down to win. That really bothers me because people start losing faith and confidence in the system."[37]

For Wyman, following the fundamental elements of democracy—including accessible, fair, and accurate elections—is not just a best practice; it's the only logical one. She feels we must approach governing in the best interests of everyone, not just the party's faithful. Collaboration is key for Secretary Benson as well: "I refuse to allow anyone to lessen my ability to do my job," she said. "They can play games, or they can collaborate with me to figure out how to ensure that their constituents—who are also mine—get served, and we create a democracy that works for everyone."

Continuing in this mission, Secretary Benson and Secretary LaRose of Ohio recently announced the formation of a new civility task force to encourage bipartisan collaboration.[38]

"As secretary of state, even though it is a partisan position and I run as a Republican, to be effective as the state's chief elections officer, I must operate in a truly nonpartisan manner in the office. For example, I do not take public positions on social issues like abortion or guns because they may be the subject of a ballot

**FairDistrictsOhio** @OhFairDistricts · Jun 18

Ohio Secretary of State Frank **LaRose** and Michigan Secretary of State Jocelyn **Benson** want their counterparts from around the country to join together in restoring **civility** in politics **and** confidence in elections.
@RickRouan @DispatchAlerts

Ohio and Michigan secretaries of state come together to encourage c...
Secretaries of state from Ohio and Michigan want their counterparts from around the country to join together in restoring civility in politics...
🔗 dispatch.com

initiative or referendum. If people knew my position on these issues, it taints the way they perceive how my staff checks those petitions. It reduces public confidence in the process," said Wyman.

Secretary Benson shared a similar sentiment on Twitter and in her book, *State Secretaries of State: Guardians of the Democratic Process.*[39] She has continued to share this perspective, stating, "I'm not always going to be the firebrand that says 'down with Republicans' because I don't believe that. I think we're all in this together, I think no party has all the solutions—that's why I love democracy, because everyone gets their voice heard."[40]

Women-sponsored policies do not enjoy the same legislative success as those of men.[41] While we have not conducted enough research to understand why this is the case, we hope that increasing women's representation

**Jocelyn Benson** ✅
@JocelynBenson

I wrote a book on the SOS. Regardless of party, the most effective SOS were advocates for voter engagement and drivers, and that is the kind of leadership I would bring to Lansing. It's why 12 current and fmr SOS from across the country endorsed my campaign. #MISOSDebate

9:12 AM · Oct 21, 2018 · Twitter Web Client

could change this outcome. More women like Wyman and Benson can make a significant difference, both in modernizing the way we vote and in the greater political landscape and public discourse.

Perhaps Secretary Wyman puts it best: "If we want to see more women in elected office—and I certainly do—we're going to have to overcome some pretty simple things, but we're going to have to do it together. And frankly, it's going to have to be other women that help because that's kind of what it takes."[42]

We can model the women of the Tuesday Club and our suffragist sisters who came before us.

## MORE WOMEN ELECTED = LEGISLATION THAT BENEFITS WOMEN IN BUSINESS AND PROFESSIONAL SPORTS

When women are elected, they introduce policies prioritizing women's issues, and these issues do not just affect women.[43] Policies designed to be more inclusive of women, whether enacted at the legislative level or in the workplace, benefit everyone. We know there are opportunities in boardrooms and C-suites across America, and even in professional sports.

According to new data released in June 2019 by the World Economic Forum, it will take 208 years before the United States reaches gender parity in the categories of economic participation and opportunity, educational attainment, health and survival, and political empowerment.[44] Those numbers

are sobering. As Melinda Gates discussed in a recent opinion piece for *USA Today*, "It is not destiny. It should be a call to action to invest, collaborate, and make faster progress a top priority."[45] According to data from PitchBook, female founders received 2.2 percent of $130 billion in venture capital funding in 2018. The number of deals completed by female founders is growing, though the percentage of money going to these companies remains stagnant as the total amount of VC investment increases. And US women as a whole still earn 20 percent less than men, according to the Institute for Women's Policy Research. The chasm widens when looking at the gender wage gap by race, age, or occupation.[46]

For female athletes, the wage gap depends on the sport. Tennis is the only professional sport where women and men earn similar pay, a hard-fought battle begun by Billie Jean King in the 1970s. Venus Williams picked up the torch into the 2000s.[47]

In March 2019, twenty-eight players from the US women's national soccer team filed a lawsuit against US Soccer.[48]

SOCCER UNITED STATES WOMEN

**USWNT files gender discrimination lawsuit against US Soccer in federal court**

Happy International Women's Day.

By Stephanie Yang | @thrace | Mar 8, 2019, 8:00am PST

**The Best Women's Soccer Team in the World Fights for Equal Pay**

As the U.S. women's national soccer team defends its World Cup title in France, its members are preparing for a courtroom battle.

GAME THEORY

**How the U.S. Government Is Failing Women's Soccer**

It's time for U.S. lawmakers to reconsider a framework that consistently undervalues female athletes.

By HAMPTON DELLINGER | June 09, 2019

*Stars and Stripes*, March 2018, By Stephanie Yang: https://www.starsandstripesfc.com/2019/3/8/18256187/uswnt-files-gender-discrimination-lawsuit-us-soccer-federal-court
*New York Times*, June 2019, By Lizzy Goodman: https://www.nytimes.com/2019/06/10/magazine/womens-soccer-inequality-pay.html
*Politico*, June 2019, By Hampton Dellinger: https://www.politico.com/magazine/story/2019/06/09/soccer-women-world-cup-227099

The issue began with pay equity, and the suit also claims that male soccer players are not only paid more, but they also have better travel accommodations and are provided better food.[49] Three months later, during the FIFA Women's World Cup, and while the US women's team was striding toward its victory, the two sides agreed to mediation to resolve the dispute.[50] Despite the parties being in a position to take a bold stance on pay equity, talks broke down in August 2019 following the women's World Cup victory.[51] US Soccer claimed that women are paid less because their games typically bring in less revenue and lower ratings, thereby bringing the mediation to a close. The USWNT will continue its fight in the courts.

Major companies are responding to the battle cries of women across the country and also addressing wage disparities. Beginning in 2019, businesses with more than one hundred employees must file reports with the Equal Employment Opportunity Commission (EEOC) that show what employees were paid in 2017 and 2018.[52] This

<          **Tweet**

**Melinda Gates** ✔
@melindagates

The @nytimes surveyed more than 100 women World Cup players from 17 countries about what they earn, how they live, and how they got where they are today. Check out this beautiful piece, complete with photos taken by the players.

We Asked, They Answered: 108 Women's World Cup Players on Their Job, Money and Sacrificin...
nytimes.com

10:55 AM · 6/20/19 · Sprinklr

data must be separated by both race and sex. This level of transparency regarding the differences in pay rates among women and people of color is especially important considering a recent Morning Consult/ASCEND poll that found that "most white women believe there is a gender pay gap but don't believe they're paid more than non-white women."[53] Companies such as Starbucks, Whole Foods, and Buffer, a social media management software firm, are all transparent about what employees are paid.

Study after study finds that diversity is good for business. Indeed, a 2018 Accenture Research study found that "if organizations succeed in creating a workforce culture that fosters equality, they will not just accelerate career advancement and pay for women, they will also improve career progress for men."[54] Cloverpop, a software company that specializes in decision-making, found "inclusive teams make better business decisions up to 87 percent of the time."[55] The Boston Consulting Group noted that companies with diverse leadership generated 19 percent more revenue than companies without diverse management teams.[56] McKinsey & Company reported that companies with women in executive positions outperformed competitors by 21 percent; the number jumped to 33 percent for companies with ethnic and cultural diversity in high leadership positions.[57]

On the heels of these studies, with a bill sponsored

by Senators Hannah-Beth Jackson and Toni Atkins, California became the first state to "require publicly traded companies to have at least one woman on their board of directors."[58] A few months later, women in the New Jersey legislature sponsored an identical bill, still in committee.[59] According to the National Conference of State Legislatures, "while the California Board Diversity law is the most binding, several other states have passed nonbinding resolutions encouraging companies to diversify their boards."[60]

Once again, electing women helps bring these issues to the forefront of our public discourse.

"We often say that you can't be what you can't see. But the truth is, you have to be what you can't see right now," said Secretary Benson. "I think a lot of times women leadership is exactly that, being what you're not seeing. And learning along the way as you go, how to ensure everything that comes doesn't deter you, making sure that no one else is defining your limitations—that no one else is defining what you are and can and can't accomplish." Research conducted by She Should Run, a nonpartisan nonprofit dedicated to helping more women run for office, revealed that "to see one woman run for office, eight women need to seriously explore the possibility."[61] This led the organization to launch a partnership with companies to build a pipeline from business to the ballot.

Michigan Governor Gretchen Whitmer recently

signed an executive order to launch a task force for Michigan women in sports aimed toward providing more opportunities for girls to play sports and for women to work in sports and to hold leadership positions in sports.[62] The task force will be led by Secretary of State Benson. She hopes that lessons learned through access to sports will migrate to other industries as more women become leaders.

# Gov. Whitmer establishes task force to support women in sports

The task force is the first of its kind on a state level.

Tuesday, June 18, 2019 12:17 p.m. EDT

*WKZO - Everything Kalamazoo,* June 2019, Dave Ramsey: https://wkzo.com/news/articles/2019/jun/18/gov-whitmer-establishes-task-force-to-support-women-in-sports/

Having more voices at the table—in the capitol, the C-suite, or the boardroom—is better for women, for men, for children, for companies, for the economy, and for the country. We're moving to a better future for everyone.

However, as Natalie Cone of the YMCA wrote in a recent blog post for Nonprofit VOTE, "Just because we see progress does not mean barriers don't exist."[63]

With more women than ever serving in the US Congress, it's imperative to keep moving forward. We've come so far already. After all, it's been only ten years since the Lilly Ledbetter Fair Pay Restoration Act provided women with pay discrimination protections.[64] It was 1998 when employers became liable for workplace sexual harassment.[65] Marital rape wasn't criminalized in all fifty states until 1993.[66] Contraception was legalized only fifty-four years ago. It was forty-eight years ago that Ruth Bader Ginsburg wrote the brief to the United States Supreme Court advocating that the protections of the Equal Protection Clause of the Fourteenth Amendment be extended to women.[67] And one hundred years ago most women could not vote.

At oral arguments during Justice Ginsburg's last case as a lawyer before becoming a Supreme Court justice and while advocating for nonoptional jury duty for women, then-Associate Justice William Rehnquist invoked a suffragist sister and asked Ginsburg, "You won't settle for putting Susan B. Anthony on the new dollar, then?" Ginsburg said she considered responding, "We won't settle for tokens," but instead opted not to answer the question.[68]

Better policies can improve voting, and outcomes, for all.

# CONCLUSION

**ON THE MORNING OF JULY 20, 1848,** Elizabeth
Cady Stanton took the stage in Seneca Falls, New York,
to speak at the first women's rights convention in the
nation's history. She had come a long way since the
tea party where she met Lucretia Mott. She had never
spoken in public, so she was nervous and could barely
be heard. She spoke softly in front of the small crowd
of men and women that included the great abolitionist
Frederick Douglass. She slowly gained her confidence,
ultimately reciting the Declaration of Sentiments: "We
hold these truths to be self-evident: that all men and

*women* are created equal." This kicked off the beginning of the women's suffrage movement, which lasted more than seven decades. It was the largest political reform movement in United States history. Women worked alongside many men to gain equal rights.

Seneca Falls kicked off the movement, but the western states moved first. Wyoming (in 1869) and Utah (in 1870) came first, granting women the right to vote through legislative action when they were territories. In 1893, Colorado was the first state to grant white women suffrage through a vote of the people. The very next year, in 1894, Colorado became the first state to have women in its state legislature, with three women elected to the Colorado House of Representatives. It would be another twenty-six years before national suffrage was achieved.

Our suffragist sisters had to think and act within the parameters of society in order to effect change. They did that in traditional ways, such as by holding protests and sit-ins, but also through meeting in small women's groups and cookbook parties. This is proof that, even then, women were savvy marketers and collaborated together for change. Women have done this throughout history, just as Deborah Given and Lilian Braude did in their original Tuesday Club and as Elizabeth Cady Stanton and Lucretia Mott did in Seneca Falls.

The women we interviewed for this book organized in similar ways. Cailyn and her friends came together in Ohio in advance of the 2018 election to ensure they were all registered. Kathy and her sorority sisters got their ballots in advance of Election Day and spent time reviewing and researching together. Debbie's political interest was spawned by visiting with her local Republican women's group.

The antiquated systems that still permeate our society make it difficult for women to participate in our voting process. Despite thinking that they were doing everything correctly and organizing in advance, Cailyn and Sarah still could not vote on Election Day. Both Cailyn and Sarah showed up as registered voters in their respective state databases, but not for the specific precinct location they were assigned on Election Day. They faced challenges when updating their voter registrations, and despite being passionate about voting and registering in advance, they still were not able to vote with a regular ballot. Almost turned away entirely, both women insisted on casting provisional ballots. Knowing not all states count or record provisional ballots, they both wondered about the fate of their ballots. We attempted to trace Sarah's and Cailyn's ballots to no avail. Confirming their worst suspicion, we believe neither ballot was recorded or counted.

Throughout this book, we have demonstrated that, as a nation, we do not make it easy even for the small percentage of those who choose to vote. We make most eligible voters opt in rather than opt out of the voting process. We see this both in states that are traditionally thought of as red and in those thought of as blue. Sarah and Cailyn experienced registration and polling location issues, and procedures were not followed. Many Americans miss the government-imposed registration deadlines, some simply because they're not aware of them. For the few who actually register, some cannot make it to their respective polling places, and some who do make it to a polling place discover that it's the wrong one. Sadly, voting-at-home options are not always available for the large number of people who cannot get to a polling place due to their job or life obligations. Or the absentee ballot arrives after Election Day, like it did for the husbands, who were bravely fighting for our nation abroad, of Secretaries Wyman and Benson.

Even for those women who, like Debbie, have an option to vote in person for ten days in advance of Election Day, the window is short and does not alleviate the burden on working women. Voting windows may not provide enough time to study candidates or issues on the ballot. Debbie also faces structural barriers that exist far in advance of Election Day due to the primary process and gerrymandering.

The inconvenience of voting limits turnout. Based on voter turnout numbers in the 2016 presidential election and the 2018 midterm election, such low turnout means 25–30 percent of voters choose representatives for 100 percent of the population. We are a no-vote country due to a web of complicated and antiquated voting policies enacted over hundreds of years. These policies exist in a framework that devalues human beings based on their gender, skin color, heritage, and religion. And these policies are perpetuated by political parties that benefit from understanding their voter bases well in advance of Election Day and benefit from protecting a loud minority.

There is less bureaucratic red tape and fewer institutional hurdles to getting a driver's license, buying an AR-15, filling a prescription for a controlled substance, and getting married than there is in some places to cast a vote for a county commissioner, a judge, a member of Congress, or president of the United States.

The barriers that exist prevent all people—men *and* women—from participating in our democracy. These barriers significantly impact women who have childcare or care-giving obligations or jobs in one of the many professions predominantly made up of women (moms, nurses, teachers, or social workers like Sarah). These jobs often do not allow time off to leave to vote.

Kathy's experience demonstrates that there is a lot more we can do to improve our voting experiences nationwide. Kathy benefits from a state that has same-day registration, thereby alleviating the challenges Sarah and Cailyn experienced. Kathy and women in Colorado, Oregon, Washington, and several other states receive their ballots three weeks in advance of Election Day—at home. Kathy also lives in a state with semi-open primaries, where she can choose which party she wants to affiliate with for the primaries. She is empowered with some choice.

In fact, the states that have already implemented many of the reforms that benefit Kathy and voters like her are the states with the highest voter turnout in the nation. Those are also the states with the highest representation of women. We believe it is that simple. Change the way we vote, and more people vote. And when more people vote, more women get elected.

More women voting impacts the makeup of the legislative body, the people who are making the laws, and what the laws are. Historically, our laws have been written and structured by men, including most of those governing elections. This is hard to swallow, given that women are more than half of the population. Women are not a special interest; we are 51 percent of the population. "Despite being 51% of the U.S., women are less than 25% of Congress," noted Melinda Gates. "I think that's outrageous."[1]

Again, this is not an issue painted red or blue. Many states are ripe for reform, including states such as Arizona, Michigan, Ohio, Pennsylvania, North Carolina, Florida, and many others. Reform is especially effective when states have champions such as Secretaries Wyman and Benson. Although they come from different political parties, Wyman and Benson believe in the election reform that strengthens democracy and improves the voting process for all.

While we have made so much progress as a nation because of the "suffrage" of those who came before us, and while we do not have exactly the same challenges that those women had in 1893, we have new and different challenges. We need to activate our communities and Tuesday Clubs to continue to make progress for our daughters and our sons, for our sisters and our brothers, for all of us. Just as Ruth Bader Ginsburg recognized that her life was made possible because of a community that agreed that she was not a token, once she got there, she recognized there was still great work to be done.

Even today, 80 percent of elected officials—at every level of government—are men.[2] Women make up only 27 percent of board seats in S&P 500 companies.[3] Women as a whole earn 20 percent less than men. Breaking it down, we calculate that white women as a whole make seventy-eight cents on the dollar compared with white males. African-American women make sixty-three cents on the dollar compared with white males. Hispanic women make fifty-three and a half cents. Ginsburg would not be proud to learn that researchers are predicting it will be "easier to go to the moon again than to close the gender parity gap in law."[4]

This issue is not new. "We want rights. The flour-merchant, the house-builder, and the postman charge us no less on account of our sex; but when we endeavor to earn money to pay all these, then, indeed, we find the difference," said Lucy Stone at Seneca Falls in 1848, a reminder that all that is old is new again.[5] Secretary Benson had it right when she said that "women are going to have to be what they can't see."

Our personal and professional success pays heavy tribute to the women who came before us. Deborah Given, the convener of the Tuesday Club, was Stephanie's great-grandmother, and Stephanie was given the middle name Lynn after Lilian Braude—who ultimately went on to be a a founding member of the first club for professional and business women in El Paso, Texas. These are the historical roots we stand on. We are bonded together through proverbial Tuesday Clubs and cookbook parties, committed to continuing to look at problems differently to advocate for change in antiquated systems.

Voting and election policies must change, and when they do those changes impact women and all voters for the better.

The voting policies we advocate for—expanded voting options, modernized registration systems, ballot delivery options, vote-at-home systems (traditionally known as no-excuse absentee voting), conveniently located vote centers, primary election reform, ranked-choice voting, the Fair Representation Act, and anti-gerrymandering laws—all support voters. Improving the voting experience for women certainly means the voting experience is improved for all. The changes to elections and voting discussed in parts 1 and 2 have helped women with both ease and convenience. We also know that there is not one single voting reform that will automatically result in parity for women. It is a combination of many reforms and how those reforms are implemented. Ultimately, the goal is to streamline the voting process and give voters more options while boosting voter confidence. It's time to stop playing games with voters and ensure these reforms are implemented correctly so that all women can vote and run for office.

Once we have more women in elected office and in the boardroom, we can begin to address other antiquated and unfair systems that also lead to a dilution in women's participation. Campaign finance, for example, is beyond the scope of this book, but it plays a very large role in election inequality. The way in which members of Congress vote on bills is also antiquated. The notion that parents with small children have to be present in Washington, DC, to vote on bills makes it difficult for moms and dads with young children. Currently, only 5 percent of women in Congress are moms to school- age children. Shouldn't we look at remote voting or other ways for a parent of young children to be engaged and run for office? Maybe if we changed the antiquated systems, we would have more moms in Congress.

Amber thought it was funny growing up when her dad used to stand on his head or walk on his hands. She finally asked him why he did this, and he said, "Don't you want to learn to see things differently?" We all need to look at things differently and reinvent policies that no longer work for everyone. When Amber took the stage at the Seneca Falls Convention on August 27, 2019, in the presence of descendants of Frederick Douglass and Elizabeth Cady Stanton, she reminded all in attendance that the barriers that exist to voting today are designed to exclude people from voting, but like our suffragist sisters and abolitionist advocates, we have the power to change that.

It's time we do this as a nation. We need to free the voting experience from partisan politics. We need to insist on officials who approach elections in a nonpartisan way and make appropriate reforms to fix some of the games that get played with the election process. As voters, we need to have high expectations: Expect a meaningful, accessible, high-integrity process when going to vote. Hold elected officials accountable if they are not committed to voting reform. One step in the right direction is better than none, and one step leads to another. Each step puts us further along on the path forward toward more inclusive, equitable voting reform.

When all people vote, we can create a better system for all.

We are stronger when we are *WE*.

# WHO VOTES, NOT WHO WINS PLAYBOOK

**IN ADDITION TO WRITING** *When Women Vote,* we wanted to also provide a practical playbook with suggested solutions for improving the voting experience. This playbook is designed for voters, for policymakers, and for election administration officials.

## FOR VOTERS

1. **Have high expectations**. You should have an awesome voting experience! Your voting experience should be fair (F), accessible (A), secure (S), transparent (T), efficient (E), and reliable (R). To

put it succinctly, the process should be FASTER. If your voting experience falls short, talk to your local election administrator, or report it to an election protection hotline or entity. You need to let your election officials know if your experience falls short of your expectations.

2.  **Advocate for change**. Resistance to change is the biggest barrier that we face in this movement. Share your voting experience with us at <u>www. whenwomenvote.org</u>, and share your experience with policy makers in your state. When politicians ask you to vote for them, ask them what they will do to improve your voting experience and the election process.

3.  **Collaborate with one another**. Just as we did for this book, as Stephanie's great-grandmother hosted the Tuesday Club, as women suffragettes hosted cookbook clubs, and as Kathy hosted sip-and-chat forums, bring your tribe together to discuss policy change, important issues, and the voting process. The more we converse about these issues, the more often we discover our commonalities and what brings us together.

4.  **Get involved**. As we interviewed women voters for this book, we found that the process was

understandably a mystery to them. The election process is complex, highly decentralized, and confusing. If you have not toured your local election office or served as a poll worker, try both. Pay attention to how the election is being run and ask questions.

## FOR POLICY MAKERS AND ELECTED OFFICIALS

1. **Election policy must be about who votes, not who wins**. Adopt this premise for every piece of legislation that you consider. If the policy doesn't improve the voting experience for *all* voters and it is not pro-voter, it will not work. Just because you won your election in a certain system does not mean that system effectively serves your constituents. Once your election is over, you represent all voters, not just those who cast a vote for you or donated to your campaign. Regardless of your party affiliation, you should advocate for fair, accessible, secure, transparent, and efficient election processes. Barriers and burdens in the election process such as restrictive voter registration deadlines, overly prescriptive residency requirements, and lack of options to vote outside of a specific time are not productive for voters and not at all efficient in terms of the procurement and funding of voting

systems, and thus they are woefully unfair to taxpayers.

2. **Focus on what's right, not who's right**. Our friend and colleague Robert Tipton wrote a book titled *What's Right, Not Who's Right*. Once we start to focus on that simple premise, we can better collaborate to solve the challenges that we face on election policy and systems. This same premise applies to any public policy issue. Read this book.

3. **Listen to your constituents**. There are various metrics, data-driven reports, surveys, and other feedback that you can utilize to ensure the system works for voters. Utilize this data to evaluate the effectiveness of the current system. Reports about the voting experience across the United States and in specific states are readily available, and reports such as Nonprofit VOTE's "America Goes to the Polls in 2018" summarize policy considerations and their impact on improving the voting experience. Listen to your constituents, respect voters, and give voters a chance.

4. **Look to who is doing it well**. It is no secret that states that have modernized their election policies and adopted pro-voter reforms are outperforming states that have not. Engagement and

turnout demonstrate how your constituents are civically involved. In 2018, turnout in the US was only 50 percent of the voting-eligible population, and that was considered a record year. That means that you were elected with maybe 25–30 percent of your constituents voting for you. However, in states that have modernized their process, eliminated confusing deadlines, streamlined the election process, developed effective technology, and continually improved, turnout was much higher. It makes sense that, just as in business, if you improve the customer's (voter's) experience, you will gain efficiencies, and you can serve more customers more effectively. Colorado modernized its voting model in 2013 and now is a leading state in terms of policy innovation, election administration, and civic engagement. Now, there is documented evidence of the positive impact this reform has had on improving the voting experience, increasing civic engagement, reducing costs, and, above all, more effectively serving voters. Now, other states look to Colorado as a model. Other states have also focused on implementing policies that improve the voting experience. Those policies include modernizing and streamlining the voter registration process, expanding convenient voting options, providing more days and more ways to vote, and creating fairness in redistricting and primary reform.

## FOR ELECTION ADMINISTRATION OFFICIALS

1. **Support your voters, connect with them, and listen to them**. You can do this specifically by collecting and analyzing customer service-related data. There is a wealth of information about sentiments from voters regarding their voting experience. Analyze that data and act on it. If you see a trend in call volume on a particular topic, or you see a high provisional ballot rate for a particular issue, or you have extremely long lines, or you see major machine failures, that means the process is not working and you should do something about it.

2. **Be transparent**. Invite voters, elected officials, the public, and the media into your operations. Offer public tours, educate the public about the process, encourage the public to watch the process, and utilize technology to increase transparency for your processes. Create an elections advisory committee and invite stakeholders to be a part of it.

3. **Be a champion for change**. After you have evaluated performance based on what you have heard from voters and from the public, advocate for change. The winning formula is to streamline the voting experience, advocate for pro-voter policies and voter-centric processes, and design and implement effective technology in order to improve the voting experience, improve internal operations, achieve greater efficiency, and improve service.

4. **Continually improve**. Too many election officials settle into a process or a procedure and leave it as it is. To truly make this process better for voters, we must utilize data and evaluate performance constantly and especially after each election. Seek to improve your processes. There is a great book by Brian Elms and J.B. Wogan called *Peak Performance: How Denver's Peak Academy is Saving Money, Boosting Morale and Just Maybe Changing the World*. Given its success, this peak performance approach is being implemented in local governments across the United States.

5. **Communicate**. Be proactive and strategic with your communication to voters. If you are not proactively communicating with voters about the process, someone else likely will, and you may

not appreciate the message. Voters need a trusted source of information, and they rely on their local election official (or state officials) for this.

## THE FORMULA

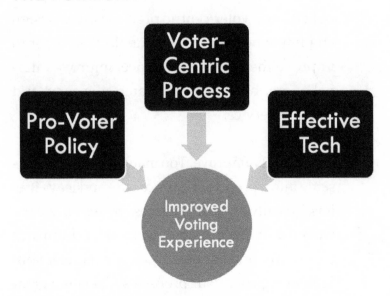

Voter-Centric Process

Pro-Voter Policy

Effective Tech

Improved Voting Experience

### POLICY RECOMMENDATIONS

1. **Modernize the voter registration process**. The more difficult and confusing the voter registration process is, the more inefficient, costly, and ineffective it is for voters, for taxpayers, and for election officials alike. Modernizing the process includes automating voter registration and address updates by utilizing government systems that are already collecting the very information that you need to register to vote. A citizen should

not have to continually complete the same forms and provide the same information repeatedly to the same governmental entities. The amount of waste this creates costs millions and millions of dollars each year. Furthermore, modernizing the process also includes eliminating confusing deadlines. States that have implemented same-day registration are seeing significant efficiencies in the process and an increase in engagement and turnout.

2. **Provide convenient options to vote**. This includes vote-at-home options while also providing in-person voting options prior to and on election day. The traditional model of the "assigned government polling location" is at best outdated. Many people commute to work, and states that force voters to an assigned location are severely limiting the ability for many voters to engage and vote. This traditional model was not designed to put voters first and meet them where they are. This is illustrated when you compare Kathy's story to Cailyn's and Sarah's stories. Thus, we believe that vote-at-home systems that are in place or being implemented in Colorado, California, Hawaii, Oregon, and Washington provide the most options for voters to engage. These systems automatically mail a ballot to a voter three to four

weeks prior to election day. These models also preserve in-person voting options prior to and on election day at vote centers. Voters can go to any vote center in the jurisdiction to vote.

3. **Set up a fair and transparent redistricting process**. The bottom line is that voters should choose their politicians and not the other way around. Both political parties have abused the redistricting process to the detriment of everyday Americans. Again, we need to change our thinking on this topic to focus on who votes, not who wins—and stop playing games with voters. Balanced participation creates balanced representation.

4. **Modernize the primary system**. Reforming the primary election process provides an opportunity to improve access, enhance fairness, and encourage more competition. Further, the primary schedule and length of time for campaigns is problematic because it creates voter fatigue and varies greatly by state. Our primary system is in need of many changes to create a more inclusive and fair process for all voters.

5. **Improve civics education**. Civics at a young age is critical to lifelong engagement. To strengthen our democracy, we must invest in civics and in

engagement at the early stages so that children understand the connection between the policy-making process and their individual and collective lives. Civics also does not stop at high school graduation. It must continue to be a lifelong, continuous learning engagement. College campuses should implement voter registration drives and strive to get 100 percent voter registration.

6. **Other reforms**. We did not discuss campaign finance reform in this book. However, it is a critical element to ensuring voters have a fair and transparent process. Currently, the campaign finance system and funding of campaigns is in conflict with putting voters first because money is so critical to success in a campaign, and thus obtaining the funds to run is prioritized over all else. This creates inequity. Further, we need to build reporting systems that provide transparency to voters and the information they may need to make informed decisions. There is also the issue of reforming the Electoral College, which is important to consider and discuss. These reforms and other ideas are often discussed in the democracy space. So, our advice is to engage and pay attention to the ideas discussed today and in the future. They matter greatly to your voting experience.

# ACKNOWLEDGMENTS

**IT TURNS OUT THAT WRITING A BOOK** is much harder than we thought, but it is also much more fulfilling than we could have imagined. Our book started with a conversation before the 2018 midterm election and built from there. We never sought to be professional authors, journalists, or writers, and we do not profess to be now. Our respect for the people who practice those trades for a living has grown exponentially. We simply had a passion for describing how we can collectively impact implicit bias in society when we change the infrastructure that was created with that bias. We focused on voting, and in particular women voters, but the concepts we explore in this book apply to many aspects of our society, many disenfranchised groups, and many systems.

We spent countless months, days, and hours writing, rewriting, editing, checking citations, and interviewing for this book. Like many women, we did much of this work while our children ran around in the background and begged for our attention—and also while we worked at our full-time jobs. We are proud that this book is not only the culmination of all of that time and effort but also the product of a friendship and partnership in sisterhood that is much bigger than any book. And like many of the women we highlight in this book, we worked together to accomplish something much bigger than each of us individually and bigger than this book—hopefully a movement. We were there for each other every step of the way—through heartbreak, illness, new beginnings, disappointment, Little League Baseball games, and the change of many seasons.

None of this would have been possible without the encouragement and support of Bob Tipton from Alden-Swain Press. Bob took a chance on us and gave us the confidence to realize our vision. He steered us to many resources and emphatically reminded us every step of the way that we had an important and timely message to deliver. While it is necessary and wonderful that women support and advance other women, collectively we cannot do it without men like Bob Tipton in our sidecar.

In addition to Bob, we want to thank the other team members from Alden-Swain Press, particularly Andrea Costantine of My Word Publishing for her leadership, Victoria Wolf of Red Wolf Marketing for the cover and interior design, and Tom Locke for his careful and precise copyediting.

Kathy Nelson, our amazing editor, ensured that each sentence advanced our narrative. She also educated us on the role of an editor, and we thank her for her patience in handling novice authors!

Thanks go to Leah Vasarhelyi for the meticulous checking of citations and making herself available on our tight schedule. We are so lucky to be a part of her bright journey ahead.

We are grateful to Amanda Tipton and Leah Charney for their early participation and for helping us get organized. They are both so talented.

The amazing, and eternally supportive, Courtney Mamuscia devoted countless hours to developing the *When Women Vote* logo and fielded texts and calls around the clock. Courtney is not only unbelievably talented, but she is also always there to help other women achieve their dreams.

Thanks go to Stuart Clubb for making, and remaking, all of the graphics throughout the book. He helped to add a visual element to the book that emphasized many of our arguments. He is an amazing visual artist!

Denver-based Effct (Adam Estacio, Uriel Berrum,

and Nick Brown) brought the content of the book to life through our website and educational video. It was a blast working with these three! And special thanks go to Kalen Acquisto for indulging us in a fun photo shoot and bringing her talent to our effort.

This book was largely made possible because of the reliable and nonpartisan data and information so graciously provided by Jennifer Morrell, Dean Logan, Cynthia Terrell, RepresentWomen, Charles Stewart III and the Election Data and Science Lab at the Massachusetts Institute of Technology, the National Vote at Home Institute, the National Conference of State Legislatures, Electionland, electionline, RepresentUs, Open Primaries, Nonprofit VOTE, the Center for Secure and Modern Elections, FairVote, the United States Elections Project, the Ranked Choice Voting Resource Center, the Center for American Women and Politics at Rutgers University, the Brennan Center, and the Pew Research Center. Thank you for ensuring we had access to all the information we needed to support our positions.

We are very lucky to be surrounded by a tribe of women (and men) across the country who dropped everything to be early readers and give us raw and honest feedback. Thanks go to Jacki Cooper Melmed, Chantell Taylor, Michelle Lucero, Rebecca Gart, Amanda Sawyer, Susan Donner, Ian Silveri, Michael Pfiefer, Cynthia Terrell, Joe Szuszwalak Jr., Lisa Stubbs, and

Andra Zeppelin. They all exemplify the sisterhood (and support from men) we write about throughout the book and are our very own virtual Tuesday Club.

Thanks go to Lele Sadoughi and her team for creating special accessories for our launch and also for lending their team and chic creative eye throughout this process. Who knew voting could be so elegantly paired with headbands!

We are also grateful to the six women we interviewed for trusting us with their stories and personal experiences: Washington Secretary of State Kim Wyman (Republican), Michigan Secretary of State Jocelyn Benson (Democrat), Sarah (Missouri), Kathy (Colorado), Cailyn (Ohio), and Debbie (Texas). Our thanks go out to them. They are forever a part of our Tuesday Club.

Together we want to thank Adam Donner for his unwavering support and commitment, not only to our friendship but to our independence as women and mothers. Thanks go to him for being an amazing dad to Adi and Marcus and also a wonderful role model to Klara and Kenton. This book would not have happened without him (and the occasional glass of wine he provided).

We are lucky in that we share a common commitment to our families and count our lucky stars every day to have them in our corner. Nothing would be possible without them. Thanks go to our parents (Susan and Stewart Forbes and Dana and Carol (Pixi) McReynolds) and our siblings (Lisa and Stephen Satter, Curtis Forbes and Melissa Heep, Amy and John Gilbert, and Michael and Sarah McReynolds) for loving and supporting us no matter what.

I am grateful to Joshua Hunt and Chelley Canales for their love, friendship, and for being my spiritual champions! (from Amber).

Finally, thanks go to all our pals, advocates, mentors, supporters, friends, and family who may not be mentioned here or who are no longer present in our lives. They are all represented throughout our work and have informed it over time. They have helped shape our careers and our minds, but mostly our hearts. We are forever changed because of the people we have had the privilege of meeting through our work and lives. Thanks go to them for believing in us, taking a chance on us, and loving us.

We are grateful!

# ABOUT THE AUTHORS

**STEPHANIE DONNER** loves to build communities and lift up other women and girls while doing so. She served as Governor John Hickenlooper's chief legal counsel and then went on to be chief legal and  people officer for Galvanize, a technology education company with eight campuses across the United States. Stephanie founded the Galvanize Foundation, a 501(c)(3) that exists to increase access to tech careers for women and people of color, and she was recognized as 9NEWS Leader of the Year in 2017 for those efforts. Stephanie is now the president of Denver's Emily Griffith Technical College, Colorado's premier trade and technical college, where she is focused on creating opportunities for all who want to learn and on driving diversity across all programs.

## AMBER MCREYNOLDS

is one of the nation's leading experts on election administration and policy, and she has spent her career improving the voting process for all. She has proven that designing pro-voter policies, creating voter-centric processes, and implementing technical innovations will improve the voting experience for all voters. Amber is now the chief executive officer for the National Vote at Home Institute and Coalition and is the former director of elections for Denver, Colorado. During her tenure, the Denver elections office was transformed into a national and international award-winning office, and she helped to lead the effort to modernize Colorado's voting process, making it a top state for voter turnout. Amber was recognized as one of ten 2018 Top Public Officials of the Year by *Governing* magazine for her transformational work to improve the voting experience.

Amber and Stephanie met during the 2013 legislative session in Colorado when they were both working on voting-modernization legislation and while they were each pregnant with a second child. They bonded over their shared commitment to ensuring that women have equal representation from the ballot box to the boardroom.

# END NOTES

## Introduction Notes

1 Penetta, Grace & Raneay, Olivia: "Today is National Voter Registration Day. The evolution of American voting rights in 242 years shows how far we've come—and how far we still have to go." *Business Insider*: Sept. 2019 https://www.businessinsider.com/when-women-got-the-right-to-vote-american-voting-rights-timeline-2018-10

2 "Congress and the Voting Rights act of 1965," *Center for Legislative Archives*: 2019. https://www.archives.gov/legislative/features/voting-rights-1965

3 Labor Force Statistics from the Current Population Survey, *Bureau of Labor Statistics*: 2018. https://www.bls.gov/cps/cpsaat11.htm

4 "Why Are Millions of Citizens Not Registered to Vote?" *Pew Charitable Trust*: 2017. https://www.pewtrusts.org/en/research-and-analysis/issue-briefs/2017/06/why-are-millions-of-citizens-not-registered-to-vote

5 "Voting and Registration in the Election of November 2016." *United States Census Bureau*. https://www.census.gov/data/tables/time-series/demo/voting-and-registration/p20-580.html

6 "American Goes to the Polls Report—2018." *Nonprofit Vote*: 2019 https://www.nonprofit-vote.org/documents/2019/03/america-goes-polls-2018.pdf/

7 Jones, Jeffrey. "Americans' Identification as Independents Back Up in 2017" Gallup, January 2018. https://news.gallup.com/poll/225056/americans-identification-independents-back-2017.aspx

8 Hill, James. "When Women Are Civically Engaged our Democracy is Stronger." *Nonprofit Vote*: March 2019. https://www.nonprofitvote.org/women-civically-engaged-democracy-stronger/

9 "2018 November General Election Turnout Rates United States Election Project." http://www.electproject.org/2018g

10 McReynolds, Amber. "Here's how North Carolina can prevent election fraud from happening again." *The Hill*: March 2019. https://thehill.com/opinion/campaign/432185-heres-how-north-carolina-can-prevent-election-fraud-from-happening-again

## *Part 1 Notes*

1 Cailyn. Interview with Authors. May 2019.

2 Hartig, Hannah. "In their own words: Why some people find voting difficult." Pew Research Center, *FactTank*: November 2018 https://www.pewresearch.org/fact-tank/2018/11/05/in-their-own-words-why-some-people-find-voting-difficult/

3 Misra, Jordan. "Voter Turnout Rates Among All Voting Age and Major Ethnic Groups Were Higher than in 2014." *US Census Bureau*: April 2019. https://www.census.gov/library/stories/2019/04/behind-2018-united-states-midterm-election-turnout.html

4 "Most Voters Have Positive Views of Their Midterm Voting Experience." *Pew Research Center*: December 2018. https://www.people-press.org/2018/12/17/most-voters-have-positive-views-of-their-midterm-voting-experiences/

5 "Voter Registration Deadlines." *National Conference of State Legislatures*: http://www.ncsl.org/research/elections-and-campaigns/voter-registration-deadlines.aspx

6 "Automatic Registration." *National Conference of State Legislatures*: http://www.ncsl.org/research/elections-and-campaigns/automatic-voter-registration.aspx

7 "Same Day Registration." *National Conference of State Legislatures*: http://www.ncsl.org/research/elections-and-campaigns/same-day-registration.aspx

8 Report by CIRCLE Staff. "Knowledge of Voting Laws Still lacking," *CIRCLE*: 2012. http://civicyouth.org/knowledge-about-voter-laws-still-lacking/

9 Cailyn. Interview with Authors. May 2019.

10 Sarah. Interview with Authors. May 2019.

11 Missouri Secretary of State. "Voter Registration Procedures." https://www.sos.mo.gov/elections/goVoteMissouri/register

12 "Voter Registration Deadlines." *National Conference of State Legislatures*: http://www.ncsl.org/research/elections-and-campaigns/voter-registration-deadlines.aspx#table%201

13 "Voter Registration Modernization." *Brennan Center*: March 2019. https://www.brennan-center.org/analysis/voter-registration-modernization-states

14 "Electronic or Online Registration." *National Conference of State Legislatures*: http://www.ncsl.org/research/elections-and-campaigns/electronic-or-online-voter-registration.aspx

15 *Texas Secretary of State Voter Registration Procedures*. September 2019. https://www.sos.state.tx.us/elections/vr/index.shtml

16 Goldenstein, Taylor. "Thousands of Online Voter Registration Applications are Invalid, Texas officials say." *Statesman*: October 2018. https://www.statesman.com/news/20181005/thousands-of-online-voter-registration-applications-are-invalid-texas-officials-say

17 "Voter Registration Deadlines." *National Conference of State Legislatures*: http://www.ncsl.org/research/elections-and-campaigns/voter-registration.aspx

18 "Automatic Voter Registration." *National Conference of State Legislatures*: http://www.ncsl.org/research/elections-and-campaigns/automatic-voter-registration.aspx

19 "Same Day Registration." *National Conference of State Legislatures*: http://www.ncsl.org/research/elections-and-campaigns/same-day-registration.aspx

20 Nonprofit VOTE and US Elections Project. "America Goes to the Polls Report 2018." *Nonprofit Vote*: March 2019. https://www.nonprofitvote.org/documents/2019/03/america-goes-polls-2018.pdf/

21 McElwee, Sean; Schaffner, Brian; Rhodes, Jesse. "How Oregon increased voter turnout more than any other state." *The Nation*: July 2017 https://www.thenation.com/article/how-oregon-increased-voter-turnout-more-than-any-other-state/

22 Nonprofit VOTE and US Elections Project. "America Goes to the Polls Report 2018." *Nonprofit Vote*: March 2019. https://www.nonprofitvote.org/documents/2019/03/america-goes-polls-2018.pdf/

23 Report by CIRCLE Staff. "Knowledge of Voting Laws Still lacking," *CIRCLE*: May 2019. https://civicyouth.org/final-analysis-of-state-by-state-youth-voter-turnout-shows-increases-across-the-country/

24 *Electronic Registration Information Center* (ERIC): https://ericstates.org/

25 *Electronic Registration Information Center* (ERIC): https://ericstates.org/

26 Torres, Kristina. "Georgia effort to clean up voter rolls underway." *Atlanta Journal-Constitution* (AJC): July 2017. https://www.ajc.com/news/state--regional-govt--politics/georgia-effort-clean-state-voter-rolls-underway/rpAkxxDXJ2LlaOXXJfioxH/

27 Judd, Alan. "Georgia effort to clean up voter rolls underway." *Atlanta Journal-Constitution* (AJC): October 2018. https://www.ajc.com/news/state--regional-govt--politics/voter-purge-begs-question-what-the-matter-with-georgia/YAFvuk3Bu95kJIMaDiDFqJ/

28 Duncan, Magdaline. "Secretary of State opposes voter registration bill despite bipartisan support." *Missourian*: April 2019. https://www.columbiamissourian.com/news/state_news/secretary-of-state-opposes-voter-registration-bill-despite-bipartisan-support/article_a4b86a7c-571a-11e9-8e6f-ef5f91374cc5.html

29 LaRose, Frank. Press Release, *Ohio Secretary of State's Office*. April 2019. https://www.sos.state.oh.us/globalassets/media-center/news/2019/2019-04-24.pdf

30 Ladd, Jonathan; Tucker, Joshua; and Kates, Sean. 2018 *American Institutional Confidence Poll.* https://bakercenter.georgetown.edu/aicpoll/

31 Rolan, Emily. " Philly voters reporting broken voting machines, long lines at polls." *Philly Voice*: November 2018. https://www.phillyvoice.com/election-voters-polling-broken-voting-booths-long-lines-midterms/

32 Dempsey, Matt; Gill, Julian; and Banks, Gabrielle. "Long lines, difficulties, at multiple polling places across Houston." *Chron*: November 2018. https://www.chron.com/news/politics/election/article/Long-lines-and-machines-down-at-multiple-polling-13366520.php

33 Horsley, Lynn; Cronkleton, Robert; and Randle, Aaron. *The Kansas City Star*: November 2018. "Here are some of the problems Kansas and Missouri voters faced on Election Day." https://www.kansascity.com/news/local/article221167130.html

34 Manskar, Noah; staff. "Ballot Scanner Breakdowns Plague NYC Voters." *Patch.com*: November 2018. https://patch.com/new-york/new-york-city/ballot-scanner-breakdowns-plague-nyc-polling-places

35 Hartig, Hannah. "Why some voters find voting difficult." *The Pew Research Center, ThinkTank*: November 2018. https://www.pewresearch.org/fact-tank/2018/11/05/in-their-own-words-why-some-people-find-voting-difficult/

36 *US Elections Project.* 2018 Turnout Data. http://www.electproject.org/2018g

37 Montellaro, Zach. "A staggering 36 million people have voted early, setting the stage for big midterm turnout." *Politico*: November 2018. https://www.politico.com/story/2018/11/05/early-voting-turnout-2018-elections-midterms-963149

38 *Washington State Legislature, Legislative Legal Services.* https://app.leg.wa.gov/RCW/default.aspx?cite=29A.40.010

39  2000 Presidential Election in Oregon. *Wikipedia*. https://en.wikipedia.org/wiki/2000_United_States_presidential_election_in_Oregon

40  "Absentee and Early Voting." *National Conference of State Legislatures*: http://www.ncsl.org/research/elections-and-campaigns/absentee-and-early-voting.aspx

41  "50 State Map" *National Vote at Home Institute*: July 2019. https://www.voteathome.org/wp-content/uploads/2019/07/50-State-Map-July-2019.png

42  "Absentee Voting By Mail." *Ohio Secretary of State*: September 2019. https://www.sos.state.oh.us/elections/voters/absentee-voting-by-mail/#gref

43  *Voter Notify Program*, Cuyahoga County, Ohio. https://boe.cuyahogacounty.us/en-US/track-my-ballot.aspx

44  "Absentee Ballot Voting." *Montana Secretary of State*. https://sosmt.gov/elections/absentee/

45  "How can Florida best brace for elections in the future? (Hint: It's in the mail)" *Miami Herald*: February 2019. http://www.tampabay.com/florida-politics/2019/02/28/how-can-florida-best-brace-for-future-elections-hint-its-in-the-mail/

46  Holdman, Raetta. "Check out your ballot before it arrives." *CBS4 Denver*. October 2018. https://denver.cbslocal.com/2018/10/10/election-day-vote-ballot/

47  Szewczyk, Jason. "How Electoral Institutions Affect Political Accountability: Evidence from All-Mail Elections." *Department of Political Science,* Emory University: June 2018. https://www.voteathome.org/wp-content/uploads/2019/01/Emory-research-into-VAH-down-ballot-impact.pdf

48  "A Colorado Congressional District Recorded the 2nd Highest Voter Turnout in the U.S." *CBS4 Denver*: November 2018. https://denver.cbslocal.com/2018/11/27/colorado-second-congressional-district-second-highest-voter-turnout/

49  2018 Voter Turnout Data. *US Elections Project*: http://www.electproject.org/2018g

50  "Colorado Voting Reforms: Early Results." *The Pew Research Center*, March 2016. https://www.pewtrusts.org/-/media/assets/2016/03/coloradovotingreformsearlyresults.pdf

51  "Absentee Voting." *North Carolina State Board of Elections*. https://www.ncsbe.gov/Voting-Options/Absentee-Voting

52  "Absentee Voting Mail" *North Carolina State Board of Elections.* https://www.ncsbe.gov/absentee-voting-mail

53  https://www.apnews.com/29cb5817cf6f4e6fbb43a4a245578d4c

54  McReynolds, Amber. "Here's how North Carolina can prevent election fraud from happening again." *The Hill*: March 2019 https://thehill.com/opinion/campaign/432185-heres-how-north-carolina-can-prevent-election-fraud-from-happening-again

55  *Texas State Election Code*: https://statutes.capitol.texas.gov/Docs/EL/pdf/EL.81.pdf

56  *Texas Secretary of State*. "Early Voting Rules." https://www.sos.state.tx.us/elections/early-voting/archive.shtml

57  Sanchez, Sarah. "Voting on Texas Election Day: When and where to vote, what's on the ballot." *El Paso Times*: November 2018. https://www.elpasotimes.com/story/news/2018/11/05/texas-election-day-2018-el-paso-voting-locations-times-ballot-results/1889513002/

58  *US Elections Project*. 2018 Voter Turnout Data. http://www.electproject.org/2018g

59  "Early Voting" *Ballotpedia*: https://ballotpedia.org/Early_voting

60  "Absentee and Early Voting." *National Conference of State Legislatures*: http://www.ncsl.org/research/elections-and-campaigns/absentee-and-early-voting.aspx#a

61  Nonprofit VOTE and ES Elections Project. "America Goes to the Polls 2018." *Nonprofit*

*VOTE*: March 2019. https://www.voteathome.org/wp-content/uploads/2019/03/america-goes-polls-2018.pdf

62 *Absentee and Early Voting*." National Conference of State Legislatures: http://www.ncsl.org/research/elections-and-campaigns/vote-centers.aspx

63 "Denver's Haul-n-Votes Mobile Voting Center Announces 2018 Primary Election Locations." *The Denver Channel*: https://www.thedenverchannel.com/news/local-news/denvers-haul-n-votes-mobile-voting-center-announces-2018-primary-election-locations-1

64 Sanders, Linley. "Missouri Counties Face Uphill Climb to Prepare for High Stakes Midterm." *ProPublica*: October 2018. https://www.propublica.org/article/missouri-counties-face-uphill-climb-to-prepare-for-high-stakes-midterm

65 *Help America Vote Act*. H.R. 3295. https://www.eac.gov/assets/1/6/HAVA41.PDF

66 Norden, Larry and McCadney, Andrea Cordova. "Voting Machines at Risk: Where We Stand Today." *Brennan Center*: March 2019. https://www.brennancenter.org/analysis/voting-machines-risk-where-we-stand-today

67 *Texas Secretary of State Release*: October 2018. https://www.sos.texas.gov/about/newsreleases/2018/102718.shtml

68 Samuels, Alex. "Here's how to avoid problems with straight-ticket voting in Texas." *Texas Tribune*: October 2018. https://www.texastribune.org/2018/10/26/texas-voting-machines-2018-straight-ticket-midterm-elections/

69 "Voting System Paper Trail Requirements." *National Conference on State Legislatures*. http://www.ncsl.org/research/elections-and-campaigns/voting-system-paper-trail-requirements.aspx

70 *Denver's Ballot TRACE System*. https://www.denvergov.org/content/denvergov/en/denver-elections-divison/voter-election-information/ballot-trace.html

71 Monahan, Kevin and Cynthia McFadden. "Has Los Angeles County just reinvented voting?" *NBC News*: May 2019. https://www.nbcnews.com/politics/2020-election/has-los-angeles-county-just-reinvented-voting-n1000761

72 Stiles, Matt. "Sweeping change is coming for L.A. County voters. If things go wrong, he'll get the blame." *LA Times*: August 2019. https://www.latimes.com/la-me-voting-ballot-dean-logan-los-angeles-county-20190609-story.html

73 Lindeman, Mark and Philip Stark. "A Gentle Introduction to Risk Limiting Audits." *IEEE Security and Privacy Special Issue*: March 2002. https://www.stat.berkeley.edu/~stark/Preprints/gentle12.pdf

74 Morrell, Jennifer. "Knowing It's Right: A Two Part Guide to Risk Limiting Audits." *Democracy Fund*, 2019 https://www.democracyfund.org/publications/knowing-its-right

75 "Piloting Risk Limiting Audits in Michigan." *Berkeley Institute for Data Science*: December 2018. https://bids.berkeley.edu/news/piloting-risk-limiting-audits-michigan

76 *Rhode Island Press Release*. "Board of Elections to conduct complex post-election audit." https://www.ri.gov/press/view/35033

77 *Georgia State Legislature*. HB 316. http://www.legis.ga.gov/legislation/en-US/Display/20192020/HB/316

78 *Florida State Senate*, CS/HB 7101. https://www.flsenate.gov/Session/Bill/2019/07101/ByVersion

79 "The public's voting values." *The Pew Research Center*: October 2018 https://www.people-press.org/2018/10/29/the-publics-voting-values/

## Part 2 Notes

1 *Open Primaries Map of States and current primary election method*. Sept: 2019. https://www.openprimaries.org/primaries_by_state

2 *Colorado SB17-305, Legislative Legal Services, Primary Election Clean-Up Bill*. May 2017. https://leg.colorado.gov/bills/sb17-305.

3 Gruber, Jeremy; Hardy, Michael A; Kresky, Harry. "Let All Voters Vote: Independents and the Expansion of Voting Rights in the United States." https://www.openprimaries.org/let_all_voters_vote_independents_and_the_expansion_of_voting_rights_in_the_united_states

4 Simon, Steve. "Presidential Primary Law Needs Fixing" *Post Bulletin*: May 2019. https://www.postbulletin.com/opinion/other_views/other-view-presidential-primary-law-needs-fixing/article_d08215b8-6845-11e9-bcaa-6b9ab2e01764.html

5 "How RCV Works" Fair Vote: 2019. https://www.fairvote.org/rcv#how_rcv_works

6 "Where Ranked Choice Voting Is Used" *Ranked Choice Voting Resource Center*: 2019. https://www.rankedchoicevoting.org/where_used

7 "Ranked Choice Voting/Instant Run-off Voting" *Fair Vote*: 2019. https://www.fairvote.org/rcv#where_is_ranked_choice_voting_used

8 Lavin, Nancy. "History is Made as Member of Congress wins seat with 'Instant Run-off." *Fair Vote*: November 2018. https://www.fairvote.org/history_is_made_as_member_of_congress_wins_seat_with_instant_runoff

9 "Campaign Civility" *Fair Vote*: 2019. https://www.fairvote.org/research_rcvcampaigncivility

10 "Women's Representation Dashboard." *Represent Women*: 2019. www.representwomen.org

11 Daley, David. "Ranked Choice Voting Is On a Roll: 6 States Have Opted In for the 2020 Democratic Primary." *In These Times*: July 2019. http://inthesetimes.com/article/21959/ranked-choice-voting-2020-democratic-primary-maine-kansas

12 Open Primaries By State Map. *Open Primaries*: August 2019. https://www.openprimaries.org/primaries_by_state

13 "A Tradition of Independence." *Washington Secretary of State's Office*. Washington: August 2019 https://www.sos.wa.gov/elections/timeline/time5.htm

14 "California Proposition 14, Top-Two Primaries Amendment." *Ballotpedia*: June 2010. https://ballotpedia.org/California_Proposition_14,_Top-Two_Primaries_Amendment_(June_2010)

15 "Unbreaking America: A NEW Short Film about Solving the Corruption Crisis" *Represent US*: 2019. https://www.youtube.com/watch?v=TfQij4aQq1k&feature=youtu.be

16 Laloggia, John. "6 Facts about US Political Independents." *Pew Research Center*: May 2019. https://www.pewresearch.org/fact-tank/2019/05/15/facts-about-us-political-independents/

17 Wheatley, Thomas. "How redrawing districts has kept Georgia incumbents in power." *Atlanta Magazine*: January 2018. https://www.atlantamagazine.com/news-culture-articles/redrawing-districts-kept-georgia-incumbents-power/

18 Totenberg, Nina. "The Supreme Court Takes Another Look at Partisan Redistricting." *National Public Radio*: March 2019. https://www.npr.org/2019/03/25/704523712/the-supreme-court-takes-another-look-at-partisan-redistricting

19 Abrams, Stacy. Post on Twitter.com: May 2019. https://twitter.com/staceyabrams/status/1125785575246696448

# PART TWO

20 *Rucho et al. v. Common Cause et al. No. 18–422.* Argued March 26, 2019—Decided June 27, 2019* https://www.supremecourt.gov/opinions/18pdf/18-422_9ol1.pdf

21 Williams, Pete. "Supreme Court Allows Gerrymandering in North Carolina, Maryland, Setting Back Reform Efforts." *NBC News*: June 2019. https://www.nbcnews.com/politics/supreme-court/supreme-court-allows-gerrymandering-north-carolina-maryland-n1014656

22 "Hogan creates Emergency Commission to Deal with Embarrassment of Gerrymandered Congressional Districts." *Washington Post*: November 2018. https://www.washingtonpost.com/local/md-politics/hogan-creates-emergency-commission-to-deal-with-embarassment-of-gerrymandered-congressional-districts/2018/11/26/0ca7dc96-f193-11e8-aeea-b85fd44449f5_story.html

23 Colorado Public Radio Staff. "Colorado Amendments Y & Z, Independent Panels For Redistricting, Have Passed." *CPR*: November 2018. https://www.cpr.org/2018/11/07/colorado-amendments-y-z-independent-panels-for-redistricting-have-passed/

24 Radio Staff. "Redistricting Proposal Passes in Michigan." *Michigan Radio, NPR*: November 2018. https://www.michiganradio.org/post/redistricting-proposal-passes-michigan

25 Rosenbaum, Jason. "Missouri Voters Backed An Anti-Gerrymandering Measure; Lawmakers Want to Undo It." *NPR*: January 2019. https://www.npr.org/2019/01/08/682979916/missouri-voters-backed-an-anti-gerrymandering-measure-lawmakers-want-to-undo-it

26 Associated Press Staff. "Redistricting Reforms Already Taking Root in Utah, Other States." *Associated Press*: June 2019. https://kutv.com/news/local/redistricting-reforms-already-taking-root-in-utah-other-states

27 Rosenbaum, Jason. "Missouri Lawmakers Want to Scrap New Redistricting System Before it Even Launches." All Things Considered, *NPR*: January 2019. https://www.npr.org/2019/01/07/683021573/missouri-lawmakers-want-to-scrap-new-redistricting-system-before-it-even-launche

28 Groft, Kyle. "The Results are In: Most Americans Want Limits on Gerrymandering." *Campaign Legal Center*: September 2017. https://campaignlegal.org/update/results-are-most-americans-want-limits-gerrymandering

29 NonProfit Vote and US Elections Project. "America Goes to the Polls Report." *NonProfit Vote*: March 2019. https://www.voteathome.org/wp-content/uploads/2019/03/america-goes-polls-2018.pdf

30 https://www.washingtonpost.com/opinions/its-up-to-voters-to-end-gerrymandering/2016/01/15/213b0e9a-ba45-11e5-b682-4bb4dd403c7d_story.html?utm_term=.1a3ae96443d8

31 Eggert, David. "Benson seeks input on redistricting reforms, eligibility." *AP News*: July 2019. https://www.apnews.com/43c5dca882654e678ff05aec686a7f28

32 Fair Vote Staff. "The Fair Representation Act." *Fair Vote*: August 2019. https://www.fairvote.org/fair_rep_in_congress#why_we_need_the_fair_representation_act

## *Part 3 Notes*

1 History. Com Editors. "Jeannette Rankin" *History.com*: October 2009. https://www.history.com/topics/womens-history/jeannette-rankin

2 Profile of Jeannette Rankin. *US House of Representatives, History, Art, and Archives.* https://history.house.gov/People/Listing/R/RANKIN,-Jeannette-(R000055)/

3 "Women Representatives and Senators by State and Territory, 1917 to Present." *US House of Representatives, History, Art, and Archives.* https://history.house.gov/Exhibitions-and-Publications/WIC/Historical-Data/Women-Representatives-and-Senators-by-State-and-Territory/

4 "Forging Lasting Institutional Change." *US House of Representatives, History, Art, and Archives.* https://history.house.gov/Exhibitions-and-Publications/WIC/Historical-Essays/Assembling-Amplifying-Ascending/Institutional-Developments/

5 Center for American Women and Politics, Eagleton Institute of Politics, Rutgers Unversity. "Current Numbers and Fact Sheets." *CAWP*: September 2019. https://www.cawp.rutgers.edu/current-numbers

6 Center for American Women and Politics, Eagleton Institute of Politics, Rutgers Unversity. "Women Elective Office 2019." *CAWP*: September 2019. https://www.cawp.rutgers.edu/women-elective-office-2019

7 *GovTrack Chart on Congressional Membership.* https://www.govtrack.us/congress/members

8 "Women's Representation and the Gender Parity Index." *Represent Women*: September 2019. https://www.representwomen.org/current-women-representation#us_overview

9 "Women in State Legislatures." *NCSL*: July 2019. http://www.ncsl.org/legislators-staff/legislators/womens-legislative-network/women-in-state-legislatures-for-2019.aspx

10 Center for American Women and Politics, Eagleton Institute of Politics, Rutgers Unversity. "Current Numbers and Fact Sheets." *CAWP*: September 2019. https://www.cawp.rutgers.edu/current-numbers

11 Current US Women's Representation. *Represent Women*: September 2019. https://www.representwomen.org/current-women-representation#us_overview

12 International Women's Representation. *Represent Women*: September 2019. https://www.representwomen.org/current-women-representation#international

13 Center for American Women and Politics, Eagleton Institute of Politics, Rutgers Unversity. "Women in State Legislatures 2019." *CAWP*: 2019. https://cawp.rutgers.edu/women-state-legislature-2019

14 Wax-Thibodeaux, Emily. "Where Women Call the Shots." *Washington Post*: May 2019 https://www.washingtonpost.com/nation/2019/05/17/nevadas-legislature-women-outnumber-men-first-nation-carson-city-may-never-be-same/

15 "Gender Parity Index by State." *Represent Women*: September 2019. https://www.representwomen.org/gpi_by_state

16 *US Census Bureau Statistics.* https://www.census.gov/quickfacts/fact/table/US/LFE046217

17 Anzia, Sarah & Berry, Christopher. "The Jackie (and Jill) Robinson Effect: Why Do Congresswomen Outperform Congressmen?" *American Journal of Political Science*: April 2011. https://doi.org/10.1111/j.1540-5907.2011.00512.x

18 Volden, C., Wiseman, A., & Wittmer, D. (2018). *Women's Issues and Their Fates in the US Congress. Political Science Research and Methods,* 6(4), 679-696. doi:10.1017/psrm.2016.32

https://www.cambridge.org/core/services/aop-cambridge-core/content/view/817B6C-136C6CC03F4A13514A93E4AAEA/S2049847016000327a.pdf/womens_issues_and_their_fates_in_the_us_congress.pdf

19 *Nevada State Legislature Bill List.* https://www.leg.state.nv.us/Session/80th2019/

20 Lochhead, Colton & Dentzer, Bill. "Nevada's First Femal Legislature Got a Lot Done." *Las Vegas Review Journal*: June 2019. https://www.reviewjournal.com/news/politics-and-government/2019-legislature/nevadas-first-female-majority-legislature-got-a-lot-done-1693390/

21 Wirthman, Lisa. "The Very Real Effects of Having Women in Office." *5280.com*: April 2019. https://www.5280.com/2019/04/the-very-real-effects-of-having-more-women-in-office/

22 *Colorado State Legislature Bill List.* https://leg.colorado.gov/bills/sb19-085

23 Colorado Public Radio Staff. "The Colorado Legislature Closed Friday. Here Are The Bills That Became Law, And Here Are The Ones Left On The Marble Cutting Room Floor." *Colorado Public Radio (CPR):* April 2019. https://www.cpr.org/news/story/the-colorado-legislature-closes-may-9-here-are-the-bills-in-progress-signed-into-law-and

24 Birkeland, Bente. "Colorado Paid Family Leave Program Bounced to Next Year." *Colorado Public Radio (CRP):* April 2019. https://www.cpr.org/news/story/Colorado-Paid-Family-Leave-Program-Bounced-To-Next-Year

25 *Colorado Legislature Bill List.* https://leg.colorado.gov/bills/hb19-1224

26 Cooney, Samantha. "This is the Last State to Not Send a Women to Congress." *Time Magazine*: March 2018. https://time.com/5207264/mississippi-women-congress/

27 Gender Parity Index—Mississippi. *Fair Vote*: September 2019. https://fairvote.app.box.com/s/figm0e08yqa34yxt81l8tt7b334ky736

28 https://www.usatoday.com/story/money/2019/02/21/average-life-expectancy-in-the-us-hawaii-top-state-for-a-long-life/39018551/

29 Center for Disease Control and Prevention. "Infant Mortality Rates by State." *National Center for Health Statistics: 2019*. https://www.cdc.gov/nchs/pressroom/sosmap/infant_mortality_rates/infant_mortality.htm

30 "Mississippi Woman Suffrage Association." *University of Mississippi Libraries Digital Collections*: 2019. http://clio.lib.olemiss.edu/cdm/landingpage/collection/suffrage

31 Milligan, Susan. "States With Largest and Smallest Gender Pay Gap." *USNews*: April 2019. https://www.usnews.com/news/best-states/articles/2019-04-02/states-with-largest-and-smallest-gender-pay-gap

32 *Indiana Secretary of State Voter Information.* https://www.in.gov/sos/elections/2402.htm

33 "America Goes to the Polls Report 2018." *NonProfit Vote and US Elections Project*: March 2019. https://www.nonprofitvote.org/documents/2019/03/america-goes-polls-2018.pdf/

34 Kathlene, Lyn. "Power and Influence in State Legsilative Policy Making: The Interaction of Gender and Position in Committee Hearing Debates." *American Political Science Review*: September 1994. https://www.jstor.org/stable/2944795?seq=1#page_scan_tab_contents

35 Miller, Claire Cain. "Women Actually Do Govern Differently." *New York Times*: November 2016. https://www.nytimes.com/2016/11/10/upshot/women-actually-do-govern-differently.html

36 Lochhead, Colton & Dentzer, Bill. "Nevada's First Femal Legislature Got a Lot Done." *Las Vegas Review Journal*: June 2019. https://www.reviewjournal.com/news/politics-and-government/2019-legislature/nevadas-first-female-majority-legislature-got-a-lot-done-1693390/

37 Wyman, Kim. Interview for *When Women Vote*. March 2019.

38 Rouan, Rick. "Ohio and Michigan secretaries of state come together to encourage civility."

*National Institute for Civil Discourse*: June 2019. https://nicd.arizona.edu/news/ohio-and-michigan-secretaries-state-come-together-encourage-civility

39 *State Secretaries of State: Guardians of the Democratic Process*; Benson, Jocelyn; Routledge; 1 edition (March 28, 2010)

40 Shechet, Ellie. "The Race to Win All Races." *Vice.com*: November 2018. https://www.vice.com/en_us/article/598neb/the-race-to-win-all-races

41 Volden, C., Wiseman, A., & Wittmer, D. (2018). Women's Issues and Their Fates in the US Congress. *Political Science Research and Methods*, 6(4), 679-696. doi:10.1017/psrm.2016.32

42 Wyman, Kim. Interview for *When Women Vote*. March 2019.

43 Volden, C., Wiseman, A., & Wittmer, D. (2018). Women's Issues and Their Fates in the US Congress. *Political Science Research and Methods*, 6(4), 679-696. doi:10.1017/psrm.2016.32 https://my.vanderbilt.edu/alanwiseman/files/2016/03/VWW_Issues_201603.pdf

44 Zahidi, Saadia. "Accelerating Gender Parity." *World Economic Forum*: June 2019. https://www.weforum.org/agenda/2019/06/accelerating-gender-gap-parity-equality-globalization-4/

45 Gates, Melinda. "Let's Not Take 208 Years to Achieve Equality for Women in America." *USAToday*: June 2019. https://www.usatoday.com/story/opinion/2019/06/21/equality-for-women-cant-wait-208-years-melinda-gates-column/1511613001/

46 "Pay Equity and Discrimination." *Institute for Women's Policy Research*: 2019. https://iwpr.org/issue/employment-education-economic-change/pay-equity-discrimination/

47 Casper, Andrea. "Examining the Gender Pay Gap in Elite Sports." https://www.witi.com/articles/1324/Examining-the-Gender-Pay-Gap-in-Elite-Sports/

48 Salam, Maya. "The Long Fight for Pay Equality in Women's Sports." *New York Times*: March 2019. https://www.nytimes.com/2019/03/11/sports/us-womens-soccer-pay.html

49 Ibid

50 DelGallo, Alicia. "USWNT, US Soccer agree to mediation in equal pay lawsuit." *Pro Soccer USA*: June 2019. https://www.prosoccerusa.com/us-soccer/womens-world-cup/uswnt-u-s-soccer-agree-to-mediation-in-equal-pay-lawsuit/

51 Das, Andrea. "Mediation Talks Between US Women's Team and US Soccer Breakdown." *New York Times*: August 2019. https://www.nytimes.com/2019/08/14/sports/uswnt-mediation-us-soccer.html

52 Nagele-Piaza, Lisa. "Employers Must Report 2017 and 2018 EEO-1 Pay Data." *SHRM*: May 2019. https://www.shrm.org/resourcesandtools/legal-and-compliance/employment-law/pages/eeo-1-pay-data-report-2017-2018.aspx

53 Piacenza, Joana. "Sisterhood in the Workplace Only Goes So Far When it Comes to Perception of Pay." *Morning Consult*: May 2019. https://morningconsult.com/2019/05/10/sisterhood-in-the-workplace-only-goes-so-far-when-it-comes-to-perceptions-of-pay/

54 Shook, Ellyn and Julie Sweet. "When She Rises We all Rise." *Accenture*: 2018. https://www.accenture.com/_acnmedia/PDF-73/Accenture-When-She-Rises-We-All-Rise.pdf

55 Larson, Erik. "Diversity + Inclusion = Better Decision-Making at Work." *Forbes*: September 2017. https://www.forbes.com/sites/eriklarson/2017/09/21/new-research-diversity-inclusion-better-decision-making-at-work/#4ecd1a4e4cbf

56 Lorenzo, Rocío, Nicole Voigt, Miki Tsusaka, Matt Krentz, and Katie Abouzahr. "How Diverse Leadership Teams Boost Innovation." *BSG*: January 2018. https://www.bcg.com/en-us/publications/2018/how-diverse-leadership-teams-boost-innovation.aspx

57 Hunt, Vivan, Lariena Lee, Sara Prince, Sundiatu Dixon-Fyle. "Delivering Through Diversity." *McKinsey & Co.:* January 2018. https://www.mckinsey.com/business-functions/organization/our-insights/delivering-through-diversity

58 Wamsley, Laurel. "California Becomes 1st State To Require Women On Corporate Boards." *NPR:* October 2018 https://www.npr.org/2018/10/01/653318005/california-becomes-1st-state-to-require-women-on-corporate-boards

59 Green, Jeff and Andrea Vittorio. "New Jersey Follows California in Measure to Add Women to Boards." *Bloomberg:* December 2018. https://www.bloomberg.com/news/articles/2018-12-21/new-jersey-follows-california-in-measure-to-add-women-to-boards

60 Hentze, Iris. "Gender Diversity on Corporate Boards: What Will 2019 Bring?" *NCSL:* January 2019. http://www.ncsl.org/blog/2019/01/04/gender-diversity-on-corporate-boards-what-will-2019-bring.aspx

61 Loos Cutraro, Erin. "We Need More Women To Consider A Run for Office and Here's How We Can Do It." *Thrive Global:* June 2019. https://thriveglobal.com/stories/we-need-more-women-to-consider-a-run-for-office-and-heres-how-we-can-do-it/

62 *Michigan Executive Order: No. 2019-16, Task Force on Women in Sports*. https://content.govdelivery.com/attachments/MIEOG/2019/06/14/file_attachments/1231042/EO%202019-16%20 Task%20Force%20on%20Women%20in%20Sports.pdf

63 Hill, James. "When Women Are Civically Engaged Our Democracy is Stronger." *NonProfit Vote*: March 2019. https://www.nonprofitvote.org/women-civically-engaged-democracy-stronger/

64 Dishman, Lydia. "Here are all the basic rights America denied to your mother and grandmother." *FastCompany:* June 2019. https://www.fastcompany.com/90360082/here-are-all-the-basic-rights-america-denied-to-your-mother-and-grandmother

65 *EEOC Harassmnet Policy*. https://www.eeoc.gov/policy/docs/harassment.html

66 Smyth, Julie Carr and Steve Karnowski. " Some states seek to close loopholes in martial rape laws." *APNews*: May 2019. https://www.apnews.com/3a11fee6d0e449ce81f-6c8a50601c687

67 "Supreme Court Decisions & Women's Rights—Milestones to Equality Breaking New Ground—Reed v. Reed, 404 U.S. 71 (1971)". *The Supreme Court Historical Society*. Retrieved February 28, 2016.

68 Von Drehle, David (July 19, 1993). "Redefining Fair With a Simple Careful Assault – Step-by-Step Strategy Produced Strides for Equal Protection". *The Washington Post*; retrieved August 24, 2009.

## Conclusion Notes

1 Gates, Melinda. Statement on *Twitter,com*. August 2019 https://twitter.com/melindagates/status/1160965960225792000

2 Terrell, Cynthia and Moses, Anne. "It's Time to Retire the 'Year of the Women.'" *Refinery29*: March 2018. https://www.refinery29.com/amp/en-us/2018/03/192817/women-running-for-office-2018-reflectus-coalition?__twitter_impression=true

3 Umoh, Ruth. "The Last All-Male Board On The S&P 500 Just Added A Female Member." *Forbes*: July 2019. https://www.forbes.com/sites/ruthumoh/2019/07/25/the-last-all-male-board-on-the-sp-500-just-added-a-female-member/#50617f01399d

4 Switzer, Jill. "It'll be easier to go to the moon again than to close the gender parity gap in law." *Above The Law*: July 2019https://abovethelaw.com/2019/07/itll-be-easier-to-go-to-the-moon-again-than-to-close-the-gender-parity-gap-in-law/

5 Lewis, Jone Johnson. "The Best Quotes from the 19th Century. Feminist Lucy Stone." *ThoughtCo*: March 2019. https://www.thoughtco.com/lucy-stone-quotes-3530202

CPSIA information can be obtained
at www.ICGtesting.com
Printed in the USA
LVHW111732280120
644935LV00004BA/497